Angel Whiskers

In loving memory of all the animals
Who have shared my journey, whose love
Has brightened my days, and who are buried
In my heart.

CONTENTS

FOREWORD XI

INTRODUCTION. XV

Remembered Cat
    George Abbe. 1

L'Envoi
    Cleveland Amory 3

Last Words to a Dumb Friend
    Thomas Hardy. 17

Dedication
    Graham R. Tomson. 21

Death of the Black Cat, Mr. Jingles
    Frances Minturn Howard. 25

Tailless Tom
    Dr. Louis J. Camuti 27

The Rainbow Bridge
    Anonymous. 35

A Leavetaking
    Jean Burden 37

Sonnet
    Margaret E. Bruner 45

Request from the Rainbow Bridge
    Constance Jenkins 47

Katinka
    Lynn Hamilton 49

My Grandmother's Cat
    Edna Dean Proctor 51

Calling Muzi (1971–1986)
    Robert Peterson 57

Purr Box
    Clement Wood 59

Remembering Baggins
    Gayle McCafferty 65

First Day in Heaven
    Bianca Bradbury 69

On the Death of a Cat, a Friend of Mine Aged Ten Years and a Half
    Christina Rossetti 71

Love, Squared
    Randolph Varney 75

In Memoriam: Leo, a Yellow Cat
    Margaret Sherwood 89

Leo to His Mistress
    Henry Dwight Sedgwick 91

Calvin: A Study of Character
    Charles Dudley Warner 93

Grimalkin: An Elegy on Peter, Aged Twelve
    Clinton Scollard 103

Charles: The Story of a Friendship
and *To a Siamese Cat*
    Michael Joseph. 107

Prayer for a Little Kitten
    Ruth M. Outwater 111

The Fireside Sphinx
    Agnes Repplier 113

The Epitaph of Felis
    John Jortin 117

In Memoriam Mrs. Snowball Pat Paw
and *A Lament for S. B. Pat Paw*
    Louisa M. Alcott. 119

Au Revoir to Smokey
    Edith B. Spaulding 123

The Muse that Mewed
    Wendy Wasserstein. 125

Epitaph for a Black Persian
    E. B. Crosswhite 135

Memoir for Mrs. Sullavan
    Bryna Untermeyer 137

Walking With Lulu in the Wood
    Naomi Lazard 151

PET LOSS RESOURCES 155

ACKNOWLEDGMENTS 157

BIBLIOGRAPHY 159

FOREWORD

BY Dr. Alice Villalobos, DVM
Director, VCA Coast Animal Hospital and Cancer Center
Hermosa Beach and Woodland Hills, California

As a veterinarian specializing in animal cancer, I have a front row perspective on the emotional impact of pet loss. We treat approximately 1,500 cats with cancer each year at Coast Animal Hospital, and each day we must deal with the fact that some of our patients will die. It never gets any easier, but I have learned the importance of letting our clients know that we recognize the unique bond they have formed with their cat and that we share in their loss. Each case represents a person, a pet, a bond, and a special relationship. My mission is to preserve the pet's quality of life and the bond between pet and owner for as long as possible.

Our beloved feline friends now occupy an estimated 54 million households. Over the centuries their role has changed from protecting our food supply from rodents, to protecting our hearts from more modern concerns such as loneliness and isolation. Cats are easy to care for and are ideal pets for people of all ages. With many people living alone with a cat as their only companion, I recognize that the cat represents perhaps the most central relationship in their life, providing companionship and unconditional love. With many cats being kept entirely indoors today, we do not lose as many kittens and young cats to contagious diseases, traffic, or other outdoor dangers. With good care, cats are living a full life span to age twenty or more.

Indeed, it is easy for cat owners to avoid thinking about the day when they must say good-bye to their beloved companion of many years. Many cats age gradually and signs of illness may not be apparent until the illness is advanced. When they face a diagnosis of cancer or other terminal disease in their cat, owners may have nowhere to turn and may look to their veterinarian for emotional support during this difficult time. In many cases, medical advances have made it possible for us to extend the cat's life for some time and maintain good quality of life, giving the owner time to prepare for the ultimate loss. In some cases it is possible to provide hospice care, where we teach the owner to administer some of the treatments at home, enabling the cat to remain in its familiar environment. This new dimension in veterinary care, which I refer to as "paws-pice," enables the pet owner to give back to the cat in some way for its years of undemanding and unconditional love. It has been my experience that during this time many pet owners form even stronger bonds with their pets, as they provide daily medications and attend to the cat's needs.

In preparing my clients for the loss of their cat, I find it very helpful to reassure them that their grief is perfectly normal and that they need not feel foolish in expressing it. I am very thankful that a resource such as *Angel Whiskers* is available, because it is like a support group contained between book covers. My clients will recognize all of their feelings expressed so eloquently by these writers both famous and unknown who loved and lost a cat. The vintage photographs allow the reader to pause throughout the book to admire the grace, beauty, and mystery of all types of cats. *Angel Whiskers* is a reflection of the beautiful bond that we share with our cat, and a wonderful addition to the literature of pet loss and healing.

INTRODUCTION

Do not stand *at my grave and weep:*
I am not there,
I do not sleep,
I am a thousand winds that blow.
I am the diamond's gilt on snow.
I am the sunlight on ripened grain,
I am the gentle autumn's rain.
When you awaken in the morning's
hush,
I am the swift uplifting rush
Of quiet birds in circled flight.
I am the soft stars that shine at night.
Do not stand at my grave and cry;
I am not there,
I did not die.
                    —*Author unknown*

This moving poem often comes to my mind when I visit the pet cemetery where my pets are buried. Their graves are on a sunny hillside, partially shaded by a graceful weeping willow tree, one of several in the park. The trees are encircled with marble benches, and I often sit for a few moments and contemplate the peacefulness of the scene. Many of the graves are elaborately decorated with small statues, stuffed animals, or plastic flowers. Pinwheels

turn in the breeze, adding a festive air. Fresh flowers mark a recent burial. Elaborately carved headstones contain photographs of the pet and sentimental epitaphs. My favorite epitaph says simply, "return to sender."

Although I always feel waves of emotion as I stand at my pets' graves, when I leave I feel cleansed somehow, because I have experienced the affirmation of the deep bonds that we form with our pets. Looking over the cemetery and seeing this affirmation of enduring love, I know that I share my loss with many other people. I am not alone.

Working through pet loss can be a lonely experience. Although recent studies confirm that cats and other pets are increasingly regarded as members of the family, many people do not understand the depth of the bonds that are formed and the genuine heartache that follows the cat's death. Most people are not prepared for the powerful emotions that they will experience, which range from anger to depression. When a human family member dies, our society provides established mourning rituals to acknowledge the grief, honor the relationship, and provide emotional support. However, when a beloved pet dies, there is often no acceptable outlet for expression of the grief and loss. You show up at work the next day. You bottle up your emotions. You feel foolish. Very few people will understand what that relationship meant to you. Few will know what to say, so they say nothing. The furry presence that filled your home, perhaps greeting you each time you returned, is gone forever. The emptiness and silence can be overwhelming. Months later, you may find a toy that was batted under a chair, just out of reach. Or you may find a photograph of your pet in a desk drawer. These poignant reminders of happier times may pierce your heart.

How can you recover from this pain and move into a place of healing? The first step, I have found, is to recognize that what you are experiencing is natural and normal. As with the death of any close family member, you will experience successive stages of grief over a period of time following the animal's death. It is impossible to predict how long or how short this process will be. Be especially kind to yourself during this difficult time. If your pet's death was preceded by an illness, you may be emotionally drained by the caretaking involved and the difficult decisions that you faced. If the pet was euthanized, you may feel guilty, or question whether it "was time." Was my pet suffering? Might another treatment have worked? You can be haunted by such questions in addition to your grief and loss.

It is essential to give yourself permission to grieve and time to grieve. Be gentle on yourself. You are dealing with a wound that can be difficult to heal because of society's lack of acknowledgment of this type of loss.

After experiencing the loss of several beloved pets in recent years, I have found that the most powerful way of healing is to affirm and to honor the bond with my pets in some tangible way. I began by reading poems and stories written by others who had also experienced this type of loss. In their poignant tributes I found an affirmation of my feelings. I also found that

the sharing of this loss was very healing. I realized that it's okay to feel sad; it's okay to have a burial service, and it's okay to have ongoing rituals such as lighting a candle in my pet's memory. I found great solace in reading poems such as "The Rainbow Bridge," about being reunited with my pets in the afterlife. I found healing in pieces "written" by the pet such as "Request from the Rainbow Bridge," in which Isolde, a Siamese cat, asks "remember not the fight for breath/remember not the strife. Please do not dwell upon my death/but celebrate my life."

The purpose of this anthology is to honor the bond with our beloved pets as a pathway to healing the pain of pet loss. Poets and writers throughout history have enjoyed the companionship and inspiration of cats and have penned these moving tributes. Perhaps you are reading this book because you have recently experienced the loss of a beloved cat. Or you may have a family member or friend whom you wish to comfort in their loss. In either case, may you find comfort, healing, and ultimately celebration of the lasting bond in these pages. The gifts of the spirit that our pets so generously give us, which include companionship, understanding, silent communication, acceptance, forgiveness, and unconditional love, are gifts that will live forever in our hearts.

——LAUREL E. HUNT
Pasadena, California
April 2000

. . . It is seemingly simple, such a companionship, depending on scarcely more than mere propinquity, a few actions, a touch of the cold, moist nose, a soft paw against the cheek, a greeting at the door, a few moments of romping, a warm soft ball of fur curled on the knee, or a long stare. It is thus that the sympathy between men and animals expresses itself, but interwoven, and collectively, these details evoke an emotion which it is very difficult even for time to destroy.

—Carl Van Vechten,
"Feathers," 1921

Angel Whiskers

Remembered Cat

GEORGE ABBE
1945

THROUGH THE LONG *orchards of a childhood*
        dream,
    Under the blossom-loaded branches of the cherry,
The hunting cat moves with a rippling gleam,
Parting the grass with muscled shoulder, rippled and furry.
Green core to golden eye, love shadowy and late
Under the hot front of that glancing look—
This is the cat that will crouch, and spring, and sate
The tendoned beast in him, and then at my gate
Will yowl with murmured penitence. I at my book
Will hear, and let him in. Then later, curling
At window ledge, the wise smile cupping the jowl,
He will murmur his sly love, letting hate
Sink down with embered glow through memory's grate,
Knowing the moon will return with freedom, with howl
Of fighters over the wild grass, and soft sound purling
Under the shadowy vines where the lovers wait.

Through all the winding years of childhood moves
This tawny cat I loved, and watched, and fed,

And heard above the sound of sleet and snow,
Prowling the world, while I lay warm in bed.
No night is dark, no swollen wind of autumn blows
Without my hearing, far, and sad, and wild—
Yet filled with all my longings, too—that cry,
Horrid and bestial, murmured, and loving, and mild—
And yet I knew, I knew though still a child
That under the shadowy gold of the fur there glowed
The lava and the molten force of worlds
That lived at time's beginning, curved my sky
With sunburst, made the heart throb in the necks of girls,
And drove me through a world of beauty hungrily.

Gold cat immortal, parting the dew-bright grass,
Crossing the windy orchards of years, hot life in your eye,
Thanks for your furtive friendship, the hours of youth
When under your savage voice sang the music of truth,
When the urge of the beast for love lay under the glass
Of your green-gold watching. Even as I
You knew the flight, the claw, the smell of blood.
Thanks for that lesson; that beauty molded in motion
And locking the hunger of flesh with the earth and the
    ocean
And all things lonely and lost under mortal sky.

L'Envoi

CLEVELAND AMORY
1993

 REMEMBER WELL—as I am sure anyone who has ever been owned by a cat always does—the first time I knew that Polar Bear was seriously ill. I remember it well, as I am sure you remember when you knew your cat was seriously ill. It is like being stabbed.

For months, I had failed to recognize signs I should have recognized—but which I always attributed to his arthritis. For one, there was his increasingly poor movement of his front legs, let alone the continuing problem of his arthritic back legs. For another, there was the matter of his lying down in an obviously not-wholly-comfortable position and not doing anything to rectify it as he surely would have in happier days. For still another, there was the matter of the doorbell ringing. For some time I had noticed that when this happened, he would go more and more slowly to it. But now I noticed there were times, even now most times, when he did not go at all. Just the same, although I recognized all of these signs and many more

I put them down, at least at first, when they were not so glaringly apparent, either to his arthritis or to his being not as young as he was. It was not hard to do—he was, after all, no longer a spring chicken, or rather I should say, as better befits a cat, a spring kitten. . . .

At the same time, something else was beginning to be very clear to me. This was that animals battle whatever infirmity or wound or disability they have with such bravery and lack of complaining that it must actually be seen to be believed. I would see that quality in Polar Bear many times that terrible Spring, and I shall never forget it. Every now and then I would hear one of his small "AEIOU's"—the sound with which I had grown so lovingly familiar—and the only difference I could notice now was that it was, a little eerily, cut short, until it sounded almost like a plain "OW." It was not, of course, but that is what it sounded like.

Anyone who has ever been in a similar position to mine, and who has seen his or her animal carry on a difficult fight, can only love and respect that animal more, particularly when you realize that it takes a very special kind of courage. It takes a courage which is very different from human courage but is, if anything, more worthy of admiration, because human courage comes at least armed with some knowledge, whereas animal courage often comes with no knowledge at all—not even, in the case of disease, knowledge of what it is they fight. . . .

Although Dr. Tierney could not have been more gentle or more considerate, I could tell from his first examination of Polar Bear, he was concerned. When he finished, I knew from the look in his eyes that the news was not good. And it certainly was not. What Polar Bear had was that dreaded age-old disease which afflicts, in their old age, so many animals—uremic poisoning, or kidney failure.

I cannot even now bring myself to go over the day after day, week after week, step by steps Dr. Tierney tested and tried—the treatments which sometimes seemed to make him suddenly better and then, equally suddenly it seemed, failed, as well as those which seemed at first, and oh so slowly, to help a little and then, just as slowly, also seemed to fail. At home, I could tell he was going steadily downhill by, if nothing else, his failing to eat. Indeed, no matter how many different foods I tried and how many different ways I tried to entice him to eat, he hardly seemed to eat at all. And, as for his drinking, the only water I had managed to get down him was water administered myself with an eyedropper.

I remember best, toward the end, the intravenous and subcutaneous infusions Dr. Tierney gave him. These infusions, which are basically a form of dialysis, at first seemed to help so much—and indeed sometimes lasted as long as to give him four good days. But then, in between the treatments, it would be three good days, and then just two. And, finally, the treatments would last—at least toward making him better—just one day. And finally, too, there came the day, just before the intravenous infusion, during which I always held him, when Dr. Tierney said quietly, "I am beginning to wonder whether we're doing the little fellow much of a favor. . . ."

Vets are not always keen on having the owners hold their animal or even being present in the same room when their animal is being put down, and the reason is that most of them have had experiences with it, which do not make it practicable—experiences ranging from hysterics to last-minute changes of mind. In my case, I was pleased that Dr. Tierney never even mentioned it. He knew, without my saying it, that not only did I want to be in the room with Polar Bear, I wanted to be holding Polar Bear. Marian, too, had her hand on him.

The first injection was an anesthetic but then, before the final one, the sodium pentobarbital, something happened which I shall never forget. Polar Bear was lying on a metal-top table, and I was holding his head with both my hands and, as I say, Marian's hands were on him too but, just before the final injection, with what must have been for him, considering his condition, incredible effort, he pushed in a kind of swimming movement on the metal directly toward me. I knew he was trying to get to me, and although Dr. Tierney was already administering the fatal shot, I bent my face down to meet that last valiant effort of his, and with both my hands hugged him as hard as I could.

In what seemed just a few seconds it was all over. Dr. Tierney did a last check. "He's gone," he said quietly. Only then did I release my hugging hold, but, as I say, I still remember that last effort of his, and I shall remember it always. I only hope that someday I shall forget that part of my memory, which tells me that I was part of doing something wrong to him, but rather there will remain only the memory that I was part of doing something, which had to be done.

Actually, leaving the room, I was good—at least I was good leaving the examination room. When I got to the outer office, however, I saw Dorsey Smith, a dear friend of mine and Polar Bear's too, who was holding her own cat in her hands. "Is it Polar Bear?"

she asked me. I nodded. But when she also asked, "Is he all right?" I could not even shake my head. Instead I did something so unknowingly, so un-Bostonian, and so un-Me—something I could not help, not even just in front of Dorsey, but with all those other patients there, too—I burst into tears. It was embarrassing, and I was ashamed, but the worst part was that, for the first time in my life that I can remember, I could not stop crying.

I wasn't too good afterwards, either. My daughter Gaea, who lives in Pittsburgh, had wanted to come to New York for a visit, although I knew she just said that so she could be with me when I lost Polar Bear. She had always been very fond of him. What she wanted to do that very afternoon, she said when I met her, was to go to see the movie *Howards End*. I knew that was something she had made up, too, because she did not want me to go back to the apartment until Marian had had a chance to remove Polar Bear's things, or at least hide them in a closet. . . .

In any case, when Gaea and I got back to the apartment, Marian was there, and she had indeed done an excellent job of removing and hiding at least most of Polar Bear's things—the basket-bed, the toys, the scratching post, his dishes, and even his litter pan. Anyone who has had to go through an animal's death—and we all do sooner or later, and many times, too, in our lives—knows what it is like to come upon a favorite toy, a favorite ball of yarn, or indeed a favorite anything, or even something which was not a favorite, but which was still his or hers. Even a dish can do it. Although, as I say, Marian had removed all his regular dishes, I still came upon much later, when neither Marian nor Gaea were there, a little dish I liked to put his nightly snacks on. I took the dish, and sat down with it in my hand. I turned it over and over, and just sat there, and kept sitting there for so long I actually fell asleep with it. It made no sense, but then, at a time like that, more things do not make sense than do. It is the first part of the miserable loneliness which lies ahead for you, because what you are still trying to do, of course, whether you know it or not, is to hold on to your animal.

But even coming across one of your animal's things is not by any means all of what you must go through. You must also go through sitting and looking and listening, and actually thinking you see or hear your animal. At such a time, even a look at one of your animal's favorite places will be too much for you and, during the first few nights, if you are anything like me, you will not only see and hear your animal before you go to sleep—if indeed you can sleep—you will even feel his paws padding on your bed and then, after that, you will dream about him. My dreams were awful— Polar Bear in trouble, and in a place where I could see

 him but could not get to him—or else me in trouble, where he could see me but for some reason would not come to me. So many dreams had just one or the other of these two plots—so similar they seemed like endless replays.

But for me the worst part was not the sitting and thinking, or the lying and sleeping, or even the dreaming—it was the simple matter of coming home and not finding him at the door. Polar Bear always seemed to know from the time I stepped out of the elevator that it was me, and he would always be walking back and forth just out of reach of the door as it swung open, and yet near enough to rub against my leg. Whereupon, always, I gave him first a pat, then a pull-up, then a hug, and finally a hold-up of him over my head. It was our ritual.

Now, of course, there was nothing. No him, no rub, no pat, no pull-up, no hug, no hold-up, no nothing.

Night after night I would come home and just walk in quickly and sit down, still in my coat. The whole apartment had, for me, become an empty nothingness. I can only describe it as living in a void. I did not want to be anywhere else, but neither did I really want to be there. It was not just that Polar Bear was not there—it was the awful, overpowering weight of knowing he was never ever going to be there again.

As I write about it all now, I realize something I did not realize then—how lucky I was compared to so many others who have to face the loss of their animal without other animal people around them. I, at least, was surrounded by animal people. There were calls and letters and cards and wires and even faxes. And they all were so completely understanding, because they had all obviously, at some time or another, been through it themselves. I remember perhaps best a card from my friend Ingrid Newkirk. "Damn them for dying so young," she wrote, in her inimitable inverse-perverse way. After reading that I laughed—the first real laugh I had had since Polar Bear died.

I compared, during this time, my good fortune in having such understanding friends as against the fortunes of those whose sadness, I knew, must often be greeted with such incredible lines as, "But after all, it

was just an animal," or even, "Why don't you just get
another?" . . .

Finally, there remains, to those who have lost an
animal, two large questions. The first of these involves
the matter of whether or not to bury your animal. I
have always believed that, as I said in the introduction
to this book, the best place to bury your animal is in
your heart. I believe that fully. At the same time, since
so many people knew Polar Bear, and wanted to know
where he would be buried, I finally gave in. I chose as
his final resting place the Fund for Animals' Black
Beauty Ranch, which, over the years, has become
home to thousands of abused or abandoned animals.
To Chris Byrne, the able manager of Black Beauty, as
well as to his extraordinary wife, Mary, fell the job of
finding the right place, the right headstone, and the
right copper plaque. They did it all wonderfully well.
The plaque is not only a lovely one, but it is in the very
center of life at the Ranch, and is also in the shade of
three trees—a place which Polar Bear loved.

In any case, to me fell the job of writing the inscription for the plaque. I did it as follows:

Beneath This Stone
Lie the Mortal Remains of
The Cat Who Came for Christmas

Beloved Polar Bear
1977—1992
'Til We Meet Again

I chose the line " 'Til We Meet Again" from the hymn "May the Good Lord Bless and Keep You." In using that line, it brought up the second large question—do animals go to heaven? I do believe that we and our animals will meet again. If we do not, and where we go is supposed to be heaven, it will not be heaven to me and it will not be where I wish to go.

I remember once having an argument with a Catholic priest. Our argument had started on the subject of cruelty to animals in general, but it soon went on into the matter of whether or not animals went to heaven. I said that I had been told that somewhere in the Bible, it said that Jesus would someday come down from heaven again, leading an army on white horses. If animals did not go to heaven, I asked the good Father, then where did the horses come from?

Unfortunately, I had the wrong man. The good Father was one who believed in the old Catholic dogma that animals have no souls. Having heard this nonsense before, I responded to it, rather crossly and at some length. I said that the Episcopal Church to which I belonged might not be as big on souls as the Catholic

Church, but if and when the good Father and I shuf-
fled off this mortal coil, and we were going to some
glorious Elysian Fields—and here I added that being
Episcopalian, I might get a little better place up there
than he did, but that Episcopalians were very demo-
cratic, and I would do the best I could for him—but
animals were not, according to him, going anywhere,
then it seemed to me all the more important that we
should at least give them a little better shakes in the
one life they did have.

I feel I won the argument—one of the very few I
believe I have ever won with someone who was far
more learned on all areas of the subject than I was.
Of course I realize our argument had not settled the
matter of whether or not animals went to heaven.
But I had at least settled something—that, if they did
not, then we owed them even more.

Certainly in just knowing Polar Bear, let alone being
owned by him, I feel I owed him more than I could
ever repay, let alone say. To me he was, and will always
be, as I said at the beginning of this book, the best cat
ever. I called him that, as I also said, in the special
moments we had together, and I will always think of
him as that.

I also wrote in the inscription on Polar Bear's monument that we will meet again. I am not deeply reli-

gious, and when the subject comes up, it usually makes me nervous. And when something makes me nervous, I am inclined to make a joke about it. Years  ago, for example, when I was working for the *Saturday Evening Post* and my job was choosing cartoons for the magazine, one of the first I chose was a drawing of two angels in heaven with one of them saying to the other, "Do you believe in the heretofore?"

Nonetheless, heretofore or hereafter aside, what I wrote on Polar Bear's monument I do believe—that we will meet again. And if I do not always believe it, I always try to believe it, because I also believe that if you try hard enough to believe something you will in time believe it. And one thing I know is that, when Polar Bear and I do meet again, the first thing I will say to him is that he is the best cat ever. And another thing I know is that, wherever we are, he will be the best cat there, too.

Last Words to a Dumb Friend

Thomas Hardy
1920

ET WAS NEVER *mourned as you,*
Purrer of the spotless hue,
Plumy tail, and wistful gaze
While you humoured our queer ways,
Or outshrilled your morning call
Up the stairs and through the hall—
Foot suspended in its fall—
While, expectant, you would stand
Arched, to meet the stroking hand;
Till your way you chose to wend
Yonder, to your tragic end.

Never another pet for me!
Let your place all vacant be;
Better blankness day by day
Than companion torn away.
Better bid his memory fade,
Better blot each mark he made,
Selfishly escape distress
By contrived forgetfulness,

Than preserve his prints to make
Every morn and eve an ache.

From the chair whereon he sat
Sweep his fur, nor wince thereat;
Rake his little pathways out
Mid the bushes roundabout;
Smooth away his talons' mark
From the claw-worn pine-tree bark,
Where he climbed as dusk embrowned,
Waiting us who loitered round.

Strange it is this speechless thing,
Subject to our mastering,
Subject for his life and food
To our gift, and time, and mood;
Timid pensioner of us Powers,
His existence ruled by ours,
Should—by crossing at a breath
Into save and shielded death,
By the merely taking hence
Of his insignificance—
Loom as largened to the sense,
Shape as part, above man's will,
Of the Imperturbable.

As a prisoner, flight debarred,
Exercising in a yard,
Still retain I, troubled, shaken,
Mean estate, by him forsaken;
And this home, which scarcely took
Impress from his little look,
By his faring to the Dim
Grows all eloquent of him.

Housemate, I can think you still
Bounding to the window-sill,
Over which I vaguely see
Your small mound beneath the tree,
Showing in the autumn shade
That you moulder where you played.

Dedication

GRAHAM R. TOMSON
1892

EAR FURRY SHADE! *In regions of the Dead,*
On pleasant plains, by murmurous waters, led;
What placid joys your brindled bosom swell!
While smiling virgins crowned with asphodel
Bring brimming bowls of milk in sacrifice,
And, passing plump and sleek, th' Elysian mice
Sport round your feet, and frisk, and glide away,
Captured at last—a not too facile prey.
Yet, with each earthly care and tremor stilled,
With every wish of cat-hood well fulfilled,
Still sometimes turn, with retrospective gaze,
To count the sweets of less luxurious days,
When you were wont to take your simple ease
Couched at my feet or stretched along my knees:
When never cloud our loving-kindness knew
(Though now and then, alas! I punished you),
Still were you fain, conciliating, bland,
With velvet cheek to change th' avenging hand.
Still would you watch, did I but chance to roam,
Supine upon the threshold of our home

Until, my brief-pace aberrations o'er,
With purrings deep you welcomed me once more.
O dearly-loved! Untimely lost!——today
An offering at your phantom feet I lay:
Purr fond applause, and take in gracious kind
This little wreath of various verses twined;
Nor, though Persephone's own Puss you be,
Let Orcus breed oblivion——of me.

Death of the Black Cat, Mr. Jingles

FRANCES MINTURN HOWARD
1958

WILL NOT *say you moved among us shade,*
But that, if shadow made itself a shape,
It would, I think, be yours.

A movement just beyond the eye's small province
Infers a presence now denied to sight.
It ripples smoothly over ankle-bone,
Arches against the knee. If I could touch
What moves outside all searching, it would be
Familiar to me, though it still elude
My conscious vision, hooding golden eyes.

String on a chain the small absurdities
We say farewell to, dying with their creature—
We, frozen in bleak immortality
Who bury one by one our little loves.
Is grace the less because it's very small?
Must elegance assume a certain scale,
Or can it flow like water on a wall?

When he with the lightest gesture flicked a beetle
From the mantle-shelf, it was a royal dismissal
Conjuring princes and their embroidered kerchiefs.
Silence, in him, took tangible dimension—
He moved in ordered triangles of space,
And all his lines flowed long and angular
Into stark hieroglyphs of pure distinction.

And too, he had that extra quality
Of rareness, that insane dimension
Of the unpredictable. He, most decorous prince,
Became afire with greed at the smell of a clam—
Or suddenly, inappropriately affectionate,
Would leap the room to blow up a snowstorm of papers,
Having acquired a taste for demonstrative love.

Where has he gone? Is there room for fur in heaven?
If cloudy angels spread their vapourous wings
It is the small particulars that build
The citadels of our identity,
And mine is dwindled by his vanished shade.

Tailless Tom

DR. LOUIS J. CAMUTI
1980

 AILLESS TOM HAS been gone a long time now, but I still see him in my mind's eye as clear as if he had only died yesterday. I see him strutting along proud as punch, his rear end with only the tiniest stump of tail on it twitching in the breeze, and I can still smile and choke up. I like to think of Tailless Tom as my cat, which he was, but he wasn't—the way the Statue of Liberty belongs to me, but it doesn't. The truth is that Tailless Tom belonged to a whole regiment, and I think every man in that regiment belonged to him.

Tailless Tom's proud way of walking might make you think he was a Manx cat, but he wasn't. He was just an ordinary brown alley cat who had lost his tail—he never told me how—in his early years before we met. That was back in the early 1930's when I first opened my hospital in Mount Vernon.

Because he was such a friendly, gregarious cat who seemed to truly like people, Tom dropped in on me one day and I showed him around my hospital, which

stood clean and empty while I waited for customers to discover me. After the tour, Tom was kind enough to accept a dish of baby beef before going on his way.

Shortly afterward, I met the lady he lived with. She dropped in for some advice about Tom. Was there any way she could stop him from bringing home the mice, moles and birds he caught? "He puts them right at my feet, Dr. Camuti, and sometimes they're still alive!"

I told her she should feel complimented. And she should be proud that her cat was such a good hunter.

She sniffed at that, and dabbed at her eyes with a lacy handkerchief. "Well, I can't stand it. I'm a very nervous woman and I find it upsetting."

The woman knew that I thought Tailless Tom was a terrific cat. That was why she called me a week later. She sounded close to hysteria. "Do you want Tom? He's yours right now. I can't take it anymore."

"What happened?"

Her voice rose, and the words came tumbling out in a wild rush. "Do you know where he is this very minute? Sitting outside the screened porch door with a snake in his mouth, and it's still alive! You have to come and get him right away, Dr. Camuti, or I'll find some other way to get rid of him. I can't have this happening anymore!"

I said I'd be right over. Sure enough, there was Tom sitting exactly where she said he was. The snake turned out to be a racer, absolutely harmless and a baby, not much larger than a big worm. Tom dropped

it at my feet. I patted his head, and the snake shot off into the grass.

I brought Tom back with me to the hospital. He immediately sensed it was his new home, and he never went back to visit his former home. I told Tom that the hospital would have to be a temporary home for him, because as my practice grew the hospital was bound to fill up with all sorts of animals, and a cat in residence just wouldn't work out. I told him that I would certainly do my darnedest to find him a good, permanent home. Tom said nothing. He just rubbed against my pants leg and purred.

With his personality, I thought I'd have no trouble in finding a home for Tailless Tom. People seemed interested when I told them about the cat's warm, friendly disposition, but when I got to the part about his talents as a hunter I lost many of them. And the one or two that asked to meet Tom didn't seem to find this tailless wonder as attractive as I did.

One day, I thought of a perfect solution. I was the commanding officer at the White Plains Armory on South Broadway. There were lots of people around over there, and Tom liked people. It would be a great home for him. There were plenty of open fields around the place so Tom would have good hunting.

Tom took to army life like a duck to water, and the men fell for him. One of the sergeants made him his own dog tag and put it on a chain around his neck. Wearing the proof of how special he was, Tom strutted more proudly than ever.

Tom's favorite time was when the 102nd Medical Regiment would move out to Camp Smith, near Peekskill, New York, for two weeks each summer. As a member of the regiment, Tom naturally went along.

As commanding officer of the Service Command at Camp Smith, one of my duties was to supply the food to the thirteen companies in the regiment. All the supply sergeants tried to give special treats to Tom as a way of pleasing me, but Tom let them know he couldn't be bought. He would just turn up his nose and march on.

Though he wasn't officially assigned to the job, Tom

made mess hall inspection his job. It was a big job, since there were eleven mess halls for the enlisted men and two for the officers, all strung out in a 400-foot line. Tom would drop by many of them two or three times a day to look things over. Obviously he had his favorite kitchens, and the men who ran them felt honored by Tom's visits. Those he ignored tried desperately to lure him over, as though Tailless Tom was in charge of bestowing some terrific award, like the Duncan Hines Seal of Approval.

Tom actually made the whole camp his command, but he would always check in at my company several times a day just to give me a rub and a purr and let me know that I still stood high in his affection. But he refused to sleep in my officer's tent.

Tom was a born diplomat. He always bedded down with the enlisted men.

When we returned from Camp Smith, Tom went back to hunting the open fields around the armory. No matter how far he wandered, he always kept the armory in his sights, and the minute he saw men gathering for a meeting, he came racing back.

Life went on for Tom at the armory for several years. And then one day, coming back from one of his field patrols, he was run over by a car right in front of the armory. It was a loss that every man felt.

There was no question about Tom's funeral. It was automatically decided that he should have a full military send-off.

I don't think there was one man attached to the armory who skipped Tom's funeral. He was placed in a small casket and buried in the front yard of the armory while a military salute was fired in his honor and taps was sounded. I looked down the line of men standing at attention as Tailless Tom went to his glory, and I could see the sun picking up wet spots on many faces. I admit the tears were running freely down my face.

Today there is a small marker on Tailless Tom's grave in the front yard of the armory. I often stop when I'm driving to pause a minute and look at Tom's grave and remember him. I can still hear the sound of his dog tag rubbing against the chain around his neck as he strutted around with his stump of tail high in the air, and all four feet marching in proud cadence. He was a great cat and a good soldier.

The Rainbow Bridge

Anonymous

DATE UNKNOWN

 HERE IS A *bridge connecting heaven and earth.*
It is called the Rainbow Bridge because of its
many colors.

Just this side of the Rainbow Bridge there is a land of
meadows,
Hills and valleys with lush green grass.
When a beloved pet dies, the pet goes to this special place.
There is always food and water and warm spring weather.
The old and frail animals are young again.
They play all day with each other.
There is only one thing missing.
They are not with their special person who loved them on
Earth.
So each day they run and play until the day comes
When one suddenly stops playing and looks up!
The nose twitches! The ears are up!
The eyes are staring! And this one suddenly runs from the
group!
You have been seen, and when you and your special friend
meet,

you take him or her into your arms and embrace.
Your face is kissed again and again and again,
and you look once more into the eyes of your trusting pet.
Then you cross the Rainbow Bridge together, never again to
  be separated.

A Leavetaking

JEAN BURDEN
1972

ODAY I SAID good-bye to Cinnamon, my ginger tabby cat, who had shared his life with me for almost thirteen years. The pain is everywhere. It was an unexpected farewell. A sudden lameness had slowed his gait, always dignified and measured, but no one anticipated the diagnosis: osteosarcoma, metastasized to the lungs. Prognosis negative. I knew the decision I had to make—as many had before me—but the kind veterinarian didn't hurry me. "I'll be glad to send the X rays to the University of California at Davis for corroboration, but I'm pretty positive that's what it is. There is already a traumatic fracture in that left leg." He left me alone in the examining room, and I wept as though I were losing my best friend. And I was.

I had had Cinnamon's mother and uncle first—for a time all three—then Cinnamon and a matching red Persian, Jason—and for the last year and a half Cinnamon and I had shared our home with Beckett, the Himalayan. We had shared so much else, too. Friends

who came (and sometimes went), but who stopped to pat with real affection the huge, shy orange cat whose only expression, according to one friend, was adoring. And all during the last years of my mother's life he had climbed into her lap, hanging over the edges, but perfectly content. Or had stood by her chair in the dining room, waiting for a tidbit that was always offered at the end of the meal. Cinnamon never begged. He was a most polite cat. Every morning he sat on the kitchen floor beside my chair as I finished breakfast, waiting for the cereal dish to be lowered to the floor for him to lap up the last few drops of cream. I never took a nap that he didn't jump up to the bed to lie down beside me, his weight hard against my leg or back, purring his quiet restrained purr, befitting an elderly gentleman whose manners were impeccable.

He was a timid cat with strangers. A party sent him scooting under the bed, where he sometimes stayed until the last unfamiliar voice was gone. He was particularly wary of deep male voices. Women made friends with him more easily. He climbed into their laps, kneading the place to make it more his, then settling his fifteen pounds on their well-pressed skirts and closing his eyes to slits. To remove him seemed profoundly ungracious, though he never made a fuss.

In the last few years of his life he slept a great deal,

either in his basket or on my bed or in the newly upholstered chair he had claimed for his own. Only when Beckett, in his kittenish enthusiasm, hopped on him from chair or couch, urging him to play tag, did he loosen up his old joints for a romp. Then the two of them tore through the house, threatening the lamps, the Oriental art objects, the candlesticks. Once, only a few months ago, I saw him race up the avocado tree, Beckett in the lead. Often such exertions brought on a fit of coughing.

But nothing marred his appetite. He was on hand night and morning for his bowl of food. He ate with his left paw, daintily lifting the food out and putting it in his mouth. If he didn't like the selection that day, he often dropped a piece into his water as silent protest. For milk he had a special miaow, and a warm bowlful was his favorite chaser to breakfast.

With children he was especially gentle, allowing the small ones to lug him around like a sack. He was so big they could hardly lift him, but if they sat on the floor he would crawl into their laps. He never scratched a person—only the dining room Oriental rug, which was his in a definitive way no one could argue with. For the scratching post he had a fine disdain.

At night he slept in the study in his wicker basket,

only climbing down when I opened the door to say good morning. His small voice, totally out of character with his bulk, replied politely, and we were ready to begin the day.

Tomorrow he won't be here to help me. When I said good-bye to him today in the doctor's office, I tried to tell him what he had meant to me for all  those years, but of course I couldn't. One can never express the full measure of love. I could only scratch him between the ears where he loved it best and kiss him there and tell him what a very special cat he had always been—the most loving, the most loyal, the most patient with my impatience, the most trusting and devoted. "You were not just a good cat," I told him, "you were a great cat, Cinnamon. And we had happy years together. Now you have fulfilled your catness. And this is the last thing I can do for you, to spare you suffering and a miserable death. That much I can do, though it breaks my heart." He looked up at my face and miaowed questioningly. I caressed his head and ears again and turned away. I couldn't see him for the tears.

In every loss are all past losses. I weep for Cinnamon, my cat, and the deaths that have gone before.

Sonnet

MARGARET E. BRUNER
1930

HERE HAVE BEEN *many cats I have loved and*
lost,
And most often of the mongrel breed;
Stray felines have a mighty power to plead,
Especially when chilled by snow and frost.
No matter if by cares I am engrossed,
Somehow I feel that I should intercede,
They seem so much like human folk in need—
Like waifs by winds of hardship roughly tossed.

I think that I should not be satisfied
In heaven with harps and wings and streets of gold,
If I should hear by chance a noise outside
Like some lost kitten crying in the cold—,
How could Saint Peter think my act a sin
If I should tiptoe out and let him in?

Request from the Rainbow Bridge

In loving memory of Isolde Jenkins

CONSTANCE JENKINS
1992

 EEP NOT FOR *me though I am gone*
Into that gentle night.
Grieve if you will, but not for long
Upon my soul's sweet flight.
I am at peace, my soul's at rest,
There is no need for tears.
For with your love I was so blessed
For all those many years.
There is no pain, I suffer not,
The fear now all is gone.
Put now these things out of your thoughts.
In your memory I live on.
Remember not my fight for breath,
Remember not the strife.
Please do not dwell upon my death,
But celebrate my life.

Katinka

LYNN HAMILTON
1952

O LOVELY KATINKA, *in what woodland Elysium*
Now do you roam far beyond the blue skies?
Katinka, the beautiful, daintily, alluring—
The great white Persian with the sea-green eyes.

The stories are legion, my fairest Katinka,
Of sylvan forests prepared for the dead;
For the children of Bast whose nine lives are ended,
A hunter's Eden awaits their light tread.
The paths of the forest are merrily guarded
By bright angel songsters of rainbow hue;
For the feline's delight they sing there forever—
May they sing their sweetest carols for you.

But a bit of my heart lies buried, Katinka,
Where I left you beneath the grasses and fern,
And though cruel to break your celestial enchantment,
I would pay a king's ransom if you could return.

My Grandmother's Cat

EDNA DEAN PROCTOR
1900

 EAUTY WAS MY grandmother's cat and the
delight of my childhood. To this far-off day
I remember her as distinctly as I do my
aunt and cousins of that household, and
even my dear grandmother herself. I know
nothing of her ancestry and am not at all sure that she
was royally bred, for she came, one chill night, a little
wanderer to the door. But a shred of blue ribbon was
clinging to her neck, and she was so pretty, and silky,
and winsome that we children at once called her
Beauty, and fancied she had strayed from some elegant
home where she had been the pet of the household,
lapping her milk from finest china and sleeping on a
cushion of down. When we had warmed, and fed, and
caressed her, we made her bed on a flannel-lined box
among our dolls, and the next morning were up
before the sun to see her, fearing her owners would
appear and carry her away. But no one arrived to
claim her, and she soon became an important member
of the family, and grew handsomer, we thought, day

by day. Her coat was gray with tiger markings, but paws and throat and nose were snowy white, and in spite of her excursions to barns and cellars her constant care kept them spotless—indeed, she was the very Venus of cats for daintiness and grace of pose and movement. To my grandmother her various attitudes had an undoubted meaning. If on a rainy day Beauty washed her face toward the west, her observant mistress would exclaim: "See, kitty is washing her face to the west. It will clear." Or, even when the sky was blue, if Beauty turned eastward for her toilet, the comment would be: "Kitty is washing her face to the east. The wind must be getting 'out' [from the sea], and a storm brewing." And when in the dusk of autumn or winter evenings Beauty ran about the room, chasing her tail or frolicking with her kittens instead of sleeping quietly by the fire as was her wont, my grandmother would look up and say: "Kitty is wild tonight. The wind will blow hard before morning." If I sometimes asked how she knew these things, the reply would be, "My mother told me when I was a little girl." Now her mother, my great-grandmother, was a distinguished personage in my eyes, having been the daughter of Captain Jonathan Prescott who commanded a company under Sir William Pepperell at the siege of Louisburg and lost his life there; and I could not question the wisdom of colonial times. Indeed, to this hour I have a lingering belief that cats can foretell the weather.

And what a mouser she was! Before her time we often heard the rats and mice in the walls, but with her presence not one dared to peep, and cupboard and pantry were unmolested. Now and then she carried her forays to hedge and orchard, and I remember one sad summer twilight that saw her bring in a slender brown bird which my grandmother said was the cuckoo we had delighted to hear in the still morning among the alders by the river. She was scolded and had no milk that night, and we never knew her to catch a bird again.

Oh to see her with her kittens! She always hid them in the hay-mows, and hunting and finding them brought us no end of excitement and pleasure. Twice a day, at least, she would come to the house to be fed, and then how we watched her returning steps, steal-ing cautiously along the path and waiting behind stack or door the better to observe her—for pussy knew perfectly well that we were eager to see her darlings, and enjoyed misleading and piquing us, we imagined, by taking devious ways.

How well I recall that summer afternoon when, soft-footed and alone, I followed her to the floor of

the barn. Just as she was about to spring to the mow she espied me, and, turning back, cunningly settled herself as if for a quiet nap in the sunny open door. Determined not to lose sight of her, I threw myself upon the fragrant hay; but in the stillness, the faint sighing of the wind, the far-off ripple of the river, the hazy outline of the hills, the wheeling swallows over-head, were blended at length in an indistinct dream, and I slept, oblivious of all. When I woke, pussy had disappeared, the sun was setting, the cows were coming from the pastures, and I could only return to the house discomfited. That particular family of kittens we never saw till a fortnight later, when the proud mother brought them in one by one, and laid them at my grandmother's feet.

What became of Beauty is as mysterious as the fate of the Dauphin. To our grief, she disappeared one November day, and we never saw her more. Sometimes we fancied she had been carried off by an admiring traveller; at others we tortured ourselves with the belief that the traditional wildcat of the north woods had devoured her. All we knew was that she had vanished; but when memory pictures that pleasant country home and the dear circle there, white-throated Beauty is always sleeping by the fire.

Calling Muzi (1971–1986)

ROBERT PETERSON
1987

 OR MOST OF *our years, Mooska, I kept you in,*
away from wars & cars.
"Cat-going-up-a-mountain," an Indian named
you. Now, so you've
gone wild, & done.

In this window you watched the neighbor's dog laze, &
hummingbirds
shimmer in fuchsia.
Here you dreamed of Taos; I'd rap your nose through the glass
& make a face.

Table you warmed, claw you honed, wisp of fur.
The comb, the talk, the whisker, the legs, the play; a late flea,
water dish, still; empty box, that silver gaze.

Where will your shy spirit, my doe, be happy to linger now?
In your final hour, by the lighthouse, long stem of pelicans
trembling west, legato.

"To be truly alive, a man should always wear a cat on his
head."
Last notes of a nocturne for your quiet, gentle ways.

Purr Box

CLEMENT WOOD
1952

 E LOVED YOU *such a lot, little sport!*
The only pet we had—with your royal Siamese
  blood,
With your lovely creamy coat, and the velvet dusky paw
And your mask—your seal-hued face, and the
Sable-splendid ears, twitching upward, like tense ears
Of a listening universe, and your eyes, a cloudy blue
When the sky was warm and light,—but at night
They woke to fire, glittering incandescent fire,
Rubies burning, flaming red.

And your tail—it was for this we picked you
From the rest. For you bore it like a plume, always
Proud, erect, alert, with its sweet and silly tip like
A furry sable hook. Twenty pounds of leaping fire
When you leapt at games with me—at a paper butterfly
That I flipped about your head on its black
Invisible cord. Somersaults, magnificent leaps—
And you caught it at the end, and we stroked your warm
Thick fur with the vigor of a storm, while you purred

Your gratitude as if your little heart would split—
Purr-box . . . little sport.

And your gorgeous outdoor grace!
We have seen you leap and catch bats swooping
Upon the wind. You've caught chipmunks—naughty rascal
Pocket gophers, star-nosed moles, rats and mice
And field mice too, snakes three times your length, and
You'd bring them each one to the house, just to show us
What you'd caught. When we let the star mole go,
And one chipmunk—sweet little fellow—
How you scolded our soft hearts!

Almost dusk, two days ago, when you miaowed
To be let out, we let you trot away for a final hunting
Round before dusk would send you back for the supper
Waiting for you, and the warm glow of the fire, and the
Warm glow in our hearts. All night long you did not come.
We called "Kitty! Kitty! Kitty!" in the tone you
Scampered to, at the front door or the back; scouted
Round your hunting ground in the vast mice-rustling yard,
And you didn't answer us . . . If you could have answered
    us!
We threw on the outdoor lights once an hour till after
Midnight; clapped our hands—your summoning signal,
Calling, "Kitty, kitty, kitty,"

And no kitty came at all. In the morning
We found why . . . Well, we cried a little bit, happiest
That you didn't suffer; sorry for the long sweet summers
And the springs and falls you'd miss, sorrier for the
Gap you left when you left us. For we loved you.
Then I left the house alone, with a spade
And with a mattock, and a box to put you in. This was all
That I could do for the friend that we'd loved so.

I took you in my arms for the last trip
You would make. So down to the lovely glade overlooking

The waterfall, where you loved to bounce and play.
Then I laid you on the brown leaves, and I shaped the
Box to fit you; tucked you in neatly and gently,
Kissed you once, and closed the box. And I found the place
I wanted—by a slim young elm tree's bole. There were
Christmas ferns beneath it, that would stay green all
The winter. And I didn't disturb the ferns, but I dug the
Hole beside them, so their fronds would cover it.

Two feet down, all cleared of rocks
And of interweaving roots. And I lowered the box
Within it. With my hands I smoothed the dirt back.
And to keep you safe forever from marauding ghouls and
Diggers, over all I placed some slabs of the hard slate
Of the hill, each one green with its living moss.
Over these, in ritual, I let sift the crisp brown leaves:
Cover him, him that we loved; cover him, him that we love.

So I gave you to the earth that had mothered
All of us, and you lie all tucked up neat and tight
Above the waterfall, under mossy rocks and ferns,
Under hemlock and gray beech, just below the slim young
Elm that will grow a hundred years, for your gay
Furred ghost to climb in bright summers I shall not see.
Birds will nest above your head, chipmunks scuttle over

Your stones, moles will almost visit you; and the
Slow and friendly roots will weave
You a living home in your warm nest underground . . .

May some friend do this for me.

Remembering Baggins

GAYLE MCCAFFERTY
1999

 SIT ON the porch as I write, on a sunny fall afternoon. I am in his courtyard, next to his garden. The rosebush I planted in his memory has grown strong and beautiful, just as he was. As the wind blows, the rose's fragrance enters my soul. I look skyward and wish for the thousandth time that I could hold him once more.

Just a tabby cat with golden-green eyes, a year-old cat that decided to adopt us. He appeared in our driveway one August afternoon, sat down with an "I'm here—feed me!" look on his face, and stayed to brighten our home for over 16 years. For me, it was a totally new experience. I had never owned a cat and actually (foolish mortal that I was) believed I didn't like cats. And now I had accepted this cat with enormous white feet, who reminded us of Bilbo Baggins in *The Hobbit*.

Baggins was a cat who never meowed or clawed—he didn't have to. One look from his serene eyes and you knew what he wanted. He loved so many things.

He especially loved to go out in the rain and then jump on the bed, soaking wet. One of his favorite perching spots was on the hood of any car in the parking lot. I used to chastise him from the window and threaten that some day he was going to get a backside of buckshot if he didn't get off, and he would lazily look back at me with a big yawn. And he was the consummate "male model." When he was 13, I took him to the mall and had him professionally photographed. The photographer said he was a better subject than any dog he had ever posed ("all in a day's work," he would shrug). He was the best dance partner I could ever want—he never squirmed in my arms, even when I did twirls and dips. In bed he was my teddy bear, with his head tucked under my chin and my arm securely around him.

He simply loved life and everyone around him, and we were richer for it.

It happened so suddenly that it took me by surprise. One day while brushing him, I noticed how bony he was becoming, and his coat seemed unkempt. The vet's diagnosis hit my heart with an icy chill . . . advanced hyperthyroid and related heart problems. The treatment options at his age were few. Medications were tried, without success. "We'll do what we can," the vet advised, "but we have to be careful of blood clots." Baggins held his own throughout the year. I began to have hope, and I left him in the care of a trusted friend while we went south over the holidays.

Then came the day I will never forget.

When we returned, we chatted with our friend on the way home from the airport. "How was Baggins?" I asked. "He's just fine, but today he was sitting in the chair and cried out with a loud meow." How strange, I thought, but dismissed it. When we got home, he

 was under the Christmas tree waiting for us. Though his eyes were serene as always, he cried out again. To my horror, I saw that he could not walk. His back legs were paralyzed. Through a blur of tears, I tried to read the veterinary emergency book, and the words "blood clot" jumped out at me. As I cradled him in a favorite towel, we began the journey to the vet.

Everything seemed to be happening as if in a bad dream: the ride, the young vet examining him so carefully and slowly, his sad eyes meeting mine as he said "it doesn't look good." After preparing the injection, he left the room to give me time to say goodbye. As I held my best friend and stared into his beautiful eyes, he already seemed to be looking into the next world. He then caught my eyes and ever so slowly gave me a wink as if to say "it's O.K., kid . . . I'll always love you."

And then he was gone.

Some say the spirit remains after a loved one has died. I believe Baggins sent me a final love song the night he died. I was sitting in the living room around 5 A.M. unable to sleep. Suddenly in the darkness, one of my music boxes began to play by itself. The tune was the love song "All I Ask of You" from *The Phantom of the Opera.* The words go: ". . . *say you'll share with me one love, one lifetime.*"

I always told him, "you're the first, and the best." Thank you, Lord, for sending him to me.

First Day in Heaven

BIANCA BRADBURY

1946

S HEAVEN ALL *you asked of it,*
O little cat? Did Peter fit
A halo for your graceless head?
Is there a quilt for your special bed,
And a bowl of cream just out of reach
Of your thieving paw? Or do They teach
You not to steal in paradise?
Does the flapping of Their wings entice?
Do you scamper and swing on a golden fence,
Or are They teaching you reverence?
And are there really golden thrones
Up there? Or do the Mighty Ones
Have nice fat chairs that you can claw
And tear and snag with an impious paw?
And do the angels understand
That a little cat in a lonely land
Still longs for a kiss and a friendly cuff?

Celestial joys are not enough.
Please, some small saint in shining white,
Hold him close in your arms tonight.

On the Death of a Cat, a Friend of Mine Aged Ten Years and a Half

CHRISTINA ROSSETTI

CA. 1870

HO SHALL TELL *the lady's grief*
When her Cat was past relief?
Who shall number the hot tears
Shed o'er her, belov'd for years?
Who shall say the dark dismay
Which her dying caused that day?

Come, ye Muses, one and all,
Come obedient to my call;
Come and mourn with tuneful breath
Each one for a separate death;
And, while you in numbers sigh,
I will sing her elegy.

Of a noble race she came,
And Grimalkin was her name.
Young and old full many a mouse
Felt the prowess of her house;

Weak and strong full many a rat
Cowered beneath her crushing pat;
And the birds around the place
Shrank from her too-close embrace.
But one night, reft of her strength,

She lay down and died at length:
Lay a kitten by her side
In whose life the mother died
Spare her life and lineage,
Guard her kitten's tender age,
And that kitten's name as wide
Shall be known as hers that died.
And whoever passes by
The poor grave where Puss doth lie,
Softly, softly let him tread
Nor disturb her narrow bed.

Love, Squared

RANDOLPH VARNEY
1999

 HY DON'T YOU take them both?" Gary, my
downstairs neighbor, had just the two kit-
tens left, twin sisters from a litter of six,
and he was trying to convince me that two
were no more trouble than one. "If they
weren't twins, I could see them going to different
homes," he said as he held them up for my inspection.
"Look, they really belong together. Like a matched
set. You don't want to break up the set, do you?"

I had to admit, it would be a shame to separate
them, and besides they were both really beautiful—
palm-sized puffs of black and white fur, soft green
eyes, and pink paw pads, front and back. So, one in
each hand, I took them upstairs to my tiny three-room
apartment. It was April 1977.

T. S. Eliot said that cats name themselves, and that
first afternoon with the kittens I understood what he
meant. I took a long critical look at the bigger one,
and with her black with white markings, it was obvi-
ous that she should be Domino, as simple as that.

In San Francisco in the seventies, it was almost a given that your apartment would be a jungle of house-plants, and I had the usual ficuses and palms growing in oversized floor pots and Boston ferns hanging from ceiling hooks. A gardener friend had given me a small pot of some exotic bamboo, and I was watching a curious kitten—also black and white—scramble up into the pot and stalk some unseen adversary in a bonsai version of jungle warfare. She'd crouch, switch her tiny tail, then pounce on nothing, and I decided then and there that Bamboo was as good a name as any.

That first day, I set up a feeding station in the kitchen near the hot water heater, installed the litter box behind the clawfoot tub in the bathroom, and laid in all the accoutrements indoor cats require: wet and dry food, clay litter, a soft brush, and a good flea comb. I had kitten-proofed the kitchen by blocking off the back of the fridge and under the stove; I closed up boxes and drawers and cupboard doors and anyplace else that might attract inquisitive whiskers. Now that we were a family, I was determined to be a good dad.

The day's activities had exhausted all three of us, and when I settled into bed with my book, two tiny souls scaled the bedspread, tiny claws gripping the chenille, delicate ears and whiskers peeking up over the edge of the mattress. They clambered up the length of me, curled themselves into the crook of my arm, and instantly fell asleep. Gary had been right— they did belong together. I knew it as I looked down at the two of them, legs, tails, and toes enlaced to the point that I couldn't tell whose appendage was whose. This was the first of a nightly ritual in which these two gently purring babies would hold me prisoner, whose sleep I could not disturb by any movement, however small.

When I met my partner, John, he scored major points by remembering the girls' names on our second date, although it would be a few months before he could tell them apart. A year later, when we decided to get a place together, my biggest regret was that I'd be taking the girls from the only house they had ever known. True, we were moving from a three-room flat to a spacious detached home, but this was the house they were born in. I finally agreed to the move, if only for the greater good.

When moving day came, John and I sequestered the girls in the bathroom until everything was set up in the new house. Once there, halfway across town, both cats at once became intrigued with the swirl of new smells, the maze of unexplored rooms, and—something entirely new—a wide windowsill overlooking a back yard. The yard immediately became their main source of entertainment, as they perched on the sill, chattering at flitting birds and rustling mice and things that humans can't see or hear. On nice days we'd open the window and the two sisters would crouch, side-by-side, tails curled first to the left, then to the right, then lashing furiously as they simultaneously spied a sparrow darting through the branches of the fig tree.

By now, John and the cats had bonded so completely that he no longer called them "your cats"; now they were ours. To them, John had become a permanent member of the family, and they accepted him as readily as they had accepted the move to a new home.

John marveled at how I could tell Bamboo's voice from Domino's, but it was easy. She had a sweet bell of a cry that was always two notes: *EH-ow!*, and she always greeted me when I came into the room: *EH-ow!* or sometimes the abbreviated *OWrr?* if it was time to eat. Her purr was musical and high, not as deep and lusty as Domino's, but with it she communicated just as much contentment. Domino, on the other hand, was more straightforward, and a simple *Mowrrr!* was suitable for most situations.

After a few years, we had saved enough for a house of our own. This place also came with a back yard, where, on nice days, we would supervise two nosy cats as they spied on the neighbors through spaces in the fence. Occasionally, when we weren't looking, they'd escape under the gate to the alley and roam just far enough to give us apoplexy. The back yard was also where we would toss pebbles to Bamboo, who would leap and catch them between her paws in mid-air. Honest. Domino would lounge all day under the same bush, emerging now and then to graze on a blade of Bermuda grass.

So in this, the last home they would know, two sweet sisters grew to middle age and then, too soon for the two guys who loved them so, to old age. Just as they had done since the day I brought them home, they still shared their food from the same bowl, groomed each other several times a day, and sought each other out to share the thousands of naps that marked the passing of their days together.

Sixteen years go by so slowly for cats, so swiftly for people. I had always wondered how I would ever cope when the time came to say goodbye. That time came when Domino could no longer get up onto the bed by herself—tiny claws no longer able to grip the chenille—and soon after that Bamboo stopped eating her food, even the shrimp that she never turned down.

The vet told us that their kidneys were failing. How could this be? They always had enjoyed great health, they still played like kittens, bounding up the stairs, ambushing one another from the top of the sofa, never missing a meal. Yet it was true. And, being twin sisters with synchronized metabolisms, their systems were deteriorating at the same rate.

For weeks we had been giving them daily infusions of saline solution, trying to lighten the load of circulatory systems that were just giving up. But after a

while even that effort was futile, and Domino, whose back legs would no longer support her, was reduced to lying on an absorbent pad to soak up her waste. Eyes that had been bright and alert were now dull and half-closed, but the message they conveyed was unmistakable: Let's get this over with, okay?

The yellow pages listed a vet who made house calls, and we made an appointment for that afternoon. John put Bamboo in the upstairs bedroom and closed the door, away from the sadness, and all day long, we lay on the floor of the den, John, Domino, and I, and waited. At four o'clock we became silent, as I cradled Domino's head and John stroked her back. I considered how this dear animal who had been so much a part of me, of us, would in a matter of minutes be gone. But she was terribly uncomfortable, I rationalized, and facilitating a quick painless death was the greatest way that we could thank her for all she had given us.

The vet, it turned out, was an old hippie with sad blue eyes, a droopy mustache, and gray hair tied in a ponytail. He smiled kindly and assured us that we were doing the right thing. First he checked her heartbeat—how odd, I thought, to be concerned with a heart that would be stilled in a matter of minutes—

then he filled a syringe with something to put her under. "The final shot isn't really painful," he said, "but this will relax her so she won't feel anything whatsoever. Do you want to say goodbye to her now?"

Say goodbye? No, I didn't want to say goodbye. I wanted my two beautiful, playful, perfect pets to be well and chasing each other from one end of the house to the other. But I bent down very close to Domino's ear, my tears soaking her soft white ruff. "My dear little girl," was all I could say. As he gave her the final shot, the vet said, "Okay, baby, run to the light." And that was it.

Bless John. He paid the man and saw him to the door. All I could do was rock and sob.

That night, Bamboo curled up on my lap as I sat at the computer, able to do little more than stare at the monitor. Suddenly, her body tensed and she went into a terrifying seizure, and there was no question she felt the loss of her sister. Alone, without her lifelong partner, her misery was made that much worse.

Bamboo's last day was even harder for us. John had been called away on a business trip that he couldn't get out of. Before he left for the airport he gave me the number where he would be and said, "Call if anything happens." Although neither of us would say it, we both knew it was time for another visit from the traveling vet. At the door, he leaned down to stroke Bamboo, knowing he was saying goodbye to her forever.

After John left, I called the traveling hippie vet and made an appointment for that afternoon. I had to go through it all over again, this time without John's loving support.

In the meantime, I tried to make her comfortable. She had stopped eating and drinking altogether a few days before, and I wondered what in the world was keeping her alive. Trying to make her more comfortable, I lined a cardboard box with a blanket and heating pad and gently laid her down in it. As I stroked her, I whispered that it wouldn't be long before she'd be with her sister, that we loved her so much, and anything else that I could think of to ease my grief, if not her pain. Then I went to take my shower and get ready for the long wait.

When I came back to her less than ten minutes later, she was gone. Overcome, I bent down to close her eyes and stroke her while she was still warm. I told her how sorry I was that she had to die alone, and it occurred to me that maybe she had waited for the moment when I was out of the room, then had just let go. I called the vet back. "I won't be needing you after all," I told him, "she took care of it herself."

There's a place in South San Francisco, sandwiched between two cemeteries for people, where you can take your pets for cremation. We put their favorite things in the box with them: a tiny sock stuffed with catnip, a felt mouse with a length of string for a tail, a soft old towel that we always used to line their travel cage when we'd take them in for their shots. We filled out some papers and were told we could come get them in a few days. John paid extra and got a special mahogany box for their ashes. "No, I want to do this for them," he said softly when I protested. We still have the ashes because, all these years later, I can't bring myself to scatter them.

For a couple of months, the house was a pretty lonely place, especially on those foggy nights when we'd slip into bed and wish there were two warm fluff balls curled up between us. In the spring, we attended a group grief counseling session at the San Francisco SPCA, where we listened to terribly sad tales of loss. One woman, while strolling the neighborhood with her beloved tabby, watched in horror as it was attacked by a dog off its leash; an elderly man wound up in a psychiatric ward, so profound was his grief at the loss of his cat. As we sat and listened, John and I had the same thought: We had been so lucky to have had 16 good years with Domino and Bamboo, and, by comparison, their deaths had been peaceful.

That very night we heard about the San Francisco SPCA's kitten foster care program and decided that, although we weren't ready emotionally to get another cat, at least we could provide a temporary home for a homeless feline family. So for that whole spring, our house was never without a mom cat and her kittens. We'd keep them until the kittens were ready for adoption, bring them back to the SPCA, and exchange them for another homeless family. In all, we fostered three consecutive cat families. It turned out to be good nurturing for the cats and great therapy for us.

By this time we were feeling that it was time for us to settle down with a new family. From the last litter that we fostered, we picked out two winners for adoption: Skipper, an adorable cross-eyed, buck-toothed tabby, and Pepper, his aloof but gorgeous tor-toise-shell sister.

We know that Skipper and Pepper will never replace Domino and Bamboo, just as no two cats will ever replace Skipper and Pepper when their time comes. If nothing else, all our cats have taught us one important truth: Unlike people, they never give a thought to their mortality until, maybe, in the last few minutes before they check out. Instead, cats live their lives as the poet Blake described it—they catch the joy as it flies.

In Memoriam: Leo, a Yellow Cat

MARGARET SHERWOOD

1913

F, TO YOUR *twilight land of dream—*
Persephone, Persephone,
Drifting with all your shadow host—
Dim sunlight comes with sudden gleam
And you lift veiled eyes to see
Slip past a little golden ghost,
That wakes a sense of springing flowers,
Of nesting birds, and lambs new-born,
Of spring astir in quickening hours,
And young blades of Demeter's corn;
For joy of that sweet glimpse of sun,
O goddess of unnumbered dead,
Give one soft touch—if only one—
To that uplifted, pleading head!
Whisper some kindly word, to bless
A wistful soul who understands
That life is but one long caress
Of gentle words and gentle hands.

Leo to His Mistress

HENRY DWIGHT SEDGWICK
ca. 1915

 EAR MISTRESS, DO *not grieve for me*
Even in such sweet poetry.
Alas! It is too late for that,
No mistress can recall her cat;
Eurydice remained a shade,
Despite the music Orpheus played;
And pleasures here outlast, I guess,
Your earthly transitoriness.

You serious denizens of Earth
Know nothing of Elysian mirth,
With other shades I play or doze,
And wash, and stretch, or rub my nose.
I hunt for mice, or take a nap
Safe in Iphigénia's lap.
At times I bite Achilles' heel
To learn if shadow heroes squeal,
And, should he turn to do me hurt,
I hide beneath Cassandra's skirt.

But should he smile, no creature bolder,
I lightly bound upon his shoulder,
Then leap to fair Electra's knee,
Or scamper with Antigone.
I chase the rolling woolen ball
Penelope has just let fall,
And crouch when Meleager's cheer
Awakes the shades of trembling deer.
I grin when Stygian boys, beguiled,
Stare after Helen, Ruin's child;
Or, should these placid pastimes fail,
I play with Cerberus' tail.
At last I purr, and sip and spatter
When kind Demeter fills my platter.

And yet, in spite of all of this,
I sometimes yearn for earthly bliss,
To hear you calling "Leo!" when
The glorious sun awakens men,
Or hear your "Good-night, Pussy" sound
When starlight falls on mortal ground;
Then, in my struggles to get free,
I almost scratch Persephone.

Calvin: A Study of Character

CHARLES DUDLEY WARNER
1882

ALVIN IS DEAD. His life, long to him, but short for the rest of us, was not marked by startling adventures, but his character was so uncommon and his qualities were so worthy of imitation that I have been asked by those who personally knew him to set down my recollections of his career.

His origin and ancestry were shrouded in mystery; even his age was a matter of pure conjecture. Although he was of the Maltese race, I have reason to suppose that he was American by birth, as he certainly was in sympathy. Calvin was given to me eight years ago by Mrs. Stowe, but she knew nothing of his age or origin. He walked into her house one day, out of the great unknown, and became at once at home, as if he had been always a friend of the family. He appeared to have artistic and literary tastes, and it was as if he had inquired at the door if that was the residence of the author of *Uncle Tom's Cabin*, and upon being assured that it was, had decided to dwell there. This is, of

course, fanciful, for his antecedents were wholly unknown; but in his time he could hardly have been in any household where he would not have heard *Uncle Tom's Cabin* talked about. When he came to Mrs. Stowe he was as large as he ever was, and apparently as old as he ever became. Yet there was in him no appearance of age; he was in the happy maturity of all his powers, and you would rather have said that in that maturity he had found the secret of perpetual youth. And it was as difficult to believe that he would ever be aged as it was to imagine that he had ever been in immature youth. There was in him a mysterious perpetuity.

After some years, when Mrs. Stowe made her winter home in Florida, Calvin came to live with us. From the first moment, he fell into the ways of the house and assumed a recognized position in the family—I say *recognized*, because after he became known he was always inquired for by visitors, and in the letters to the other members of the family he always received a message. Although the least obtrusive of beings, his individuality always made itself felt . . .

I hesitate a little to speak of his capacity for friendship and the affectionateness of his nature, for I know from his own reserve that he would not care to have it much talked about. We understood each other perfectly, but he never made any fuss about it; when I spoke his name and snapped my fingers he came to me; when I returned home at night he was pretty sure to be waiting for me near the gate, and would rise and saunter along the walk, as if his being there were purely accidental—so shy was he commonly of showing feeling; and when I opened the door he never rushed in, like a cat, but loitered and lounged, as if he had had no intention of going in, but would condescend to. And yet the fact was, he knew dinner was ready, and he was bound to be there. He kept the run of dinner-time. It happened sometimes, during our absence in the summer, that dinner would be early, and Calvin, walking about the grounds, missed it and came in late. But he never made a mistake the second day. There was one thing he never did—he never rushed through an open doorway. He never forgot his dignity. If he had asked to have the door opened, and was eager to go out, he always went deliberately; I can see him now, standing on the sill, looking about at the sky as if he was thinking whether it were worth while to take an umbrella, until he was near having his tail shut in.

His friendship was rather constant than demonstrative. When we returned from an absence of nearly two years, Calvin welcomed us with evident pleasure, but showed his satisfaction rather by tranquil happiness than by fuming about. He had the faculty of making us glad to get home. It was his constancy that was so attractive. He liked companionship, but he wouldn't be petted, or fussed over, or sit in anyone's lap a moment; he always extricated himself from such familiarity with dignity and with no show of temper. If there was any petting to be done, however, he chose to do it. Often he would sit looking at me, and then, moved by a delicate affection, come and pull at my coat and sleeve until he could touch my face with his nose, and then go away contented. He had a habit of coming to my study in the morning, sitting quietly by my side or on the table for hours, watching the pen run over the paper, occasionally swinging his tail round for a blotter, and then going to sleep among the papers by the inkstand. Or, more rarely, he would watch the writing from a perch on my shoulder. Writing always interested him, and, until he understood it, he wanted to hold the pen. . . .

As I look back upon it, Calvin's life seems to me a fortunate one, for it was natural and unforced. He ate when he was hungry, slept when he was sleepy, and enjoyed existence to the very tips of his toes and the end of his expressive and slow-moving tail. He delighted to roam about the garden and stroll among the trees, and to lie on the green grass and luxuriate

in all the sweet influences of summer. You could never accuse him of idleness, and yet he knew the secret of repose. The poet who wrote so prettily of him that his little life was rounded with a sleep understated his felicity; it was rounded with a good many. His conscience never seemed to interfere with his slumbers. In fact, he had good habits and a contented mind. I can see him now walk in at the study door, sit down by my chair, bring his tail artistically about his feet, and look up at me with unspeakable happiness in his handsome face. I often thought that he felt the dumb limitation which denied him the power of language. But since he was denied speech, he scorned the inarticulate mouthings of the lower animals. The vulgar mewing and yowling of the cat species was beneath him; he sometimes uttered a sort of articulate and well-bred ejaculation, when he wished to call attention to something that he considered remarkable, or to some want of his, but he never went whining about. He would sit for hours at a closed window, when he desired to enter, without a murmur, and when it was opened he never admitted that he had been impatient by "bolting" in. Though speech he had not, and the unpleasant kind of utterance given to his race he would not use, he had a mighty power of purr to express his measureless content with congenial society. There was in him a musical organ with stops of varied power and expression, upon which I have no doubt he could have performed Scarlatti's celebrated cat's-fugue.

Whether Calvin died of old age, or was carried off by one of the diseases incident to youth, it is impossible to say; for his departure was as quiet as his advent was mysterious. I only know that he appeared to us in this world in his perfect stature and beauty, and that after a time, like Lohengrin, he withdrew. In his illness there was nothing more to be regretted than in all his blameless life. I suppose there never was an illness that had more of dignity and sweetness and resignation in it. It came on gradually, in a kind of listlessness and want of appetite. An alarming symptom was his preference for the warmth of a furnace register to the lively sparkle of the open wood fire. Whatever pain he suffered, he bore it in silence, and seemed only anxious not to obtrude his malady. We tempted him with the delicacies of the season, but it soon became impossible for him to eat, and for two weeks he ate or drank scarcely anything. Sometimes he made an effort to pleasure us. The neighbors—and I am convinced that the advice of neighbors is never good for anything—suggested catnip. He wouldn't even smell it. We had the attendance of an amateur practitioner of medicine, whose real office was the cure of souls, but nothing touched his case. He took what was offered, but it was with the air of one to whom the time for pellets was past. He sat or lay day after day almost motionless, never once making a display of those vulgar convulsions or contortions of pain which are so disagreeable to society. His favorite place was on the brightest spot of a Smyrna rug by the conservatory, where the sunlight fell and he could hear the fountain play. If we went to him and exhibited our interest in his condition, he always purred in recognition of our sympathy. And when I spoke his name, he looked up with an expression that said, "I understand it, old fellow, but it's no use." He was to all who came to visit him a model of calmness and patience in affliction.

I was absent from home at the last, but heard by daily postal-card of his failing condition, and never again saw him alive. One sunny morning, he rose from his rug, went into the conservatory (he was very thin then), walked around it deliberately, looking at all the plants he knew, and then went to the bay-window in the dining-room, and stood a long time looking out upon the little field, now brown and sere, and toward the garden, where perhaps the happiest hours of his life had been spent. It was a last look. He turned and walked away, laid himself down upon the bright spot in the rug, and quietly died.

It is not too much to say that a little shock went through the neighborhood when it was known that Calvin was dead, so marked was his individuality; and his friends, one after another came in to see him. There was no sentimental nonsense about his obsequies; it was felt that any parade would have been distasteful to him. John, who acted as undertaker, prepared a candle-box for him, and I believe assumed a professional decorum; but there may have been the usual levity underneath, for I heard that he remarked in the kitchen that it was the "driest wake he ever attended." Everybody, however, felt a fondness for Calvin, and regarded him with a certain respect. Between him and Bertha there existed a great friendship, and she apprehended his nature: she used to say that sometimes she was afraid of him, he looked at her so intelligently; she was never certain that he was what he appeared to be.

When I returned they had laid Calvin on a table in an upper chamber by an open window. It was February. He reposed in a candle-box, lined about the edge with evergreen, and at his head stood a little wine-glass with flowers. He lay with his head tucked down in his arms—a favorite position of his before the fire—as if asleep in the comfort of his soft and exquisite fur. It was the involuntary exclamation of those who saw him, "How natural he looks!" As for myself, I said nothing. John buried him under the twin hawthorn trees—one white and the other pink—in a spot where Calvin was fond of lying and listening to the hum of summer insects and the twitter of birds.

Perhaps I have failed to make appear the individuality of character that was so evident to those who knew him. At any rate, I have set down nothing concerning him but the literal truth. He was always a mystery. I did not know whence he came; I do not know whither he was gone. I would not weave one spray of falsehood in the wreath I lay upon his grave.

Grimalkin: An Elegy on Peter, Aged Twelve

CLINTON SCOLLARD
ca. 1900

I N VAIN THE *kindly call: in vain*
The plate for which thou once wast fain
At morn and noon and daylight's wane,
    O King of mousers.
No more I hear thee purr and purr
As in the frolic days that were,
When thou didst rub thy velvet fur
    Against my trousers.

How empty are the places where
Thou erst wert frankly debonair,
Not dreamed a dream of feline care,
    A capering kitten.
The sunny haunts where, grown a cat,
You pondered this, considered that,
The cushioned chair, the rug, the mat,
    By firelight smitten.

Although of few thou stoodst in dread,
How well thou knew a friendly tread,
And what upon thy back and head
        The stroking hand meant.
A passing scent could keenly wake
Thy eagerness for chop or steak,
Yet, Puss, how rarely didst thou break
        The eighth commandment.

Though brief thy life, a little span
Of days compared with that of man,
The time allotted to thee ran
        In smoother metre.

Now with the warm earth o'er thy breast,
O wisest of thy kind and best,
Forever mayst thou softly rest,
        In pace, Peter.

Charles: The Story of a Friendship (excerpt)

MICHAEL JOSEPH
1952

"W HEN THE DAY comes for Bunny or Coney to break my heart again," Eleanor Farjeon wrote to me, "I shall tell myself this—for more than nine years I have been able to give to a living thing I love the most perfect life possible for a cat to have. It is something that, with all our hearts and wills, we cannot do for our children, whose growing-up and discovery of life is beyond all our longing to keep them happy. You can tell yourself that for nearly thirteen years all Charles's needs of love and care and comfort were perfectly filled by you . . . There will always be other beloved ones of the Company for you to give to and take from, but I know how even that Company is a hierarchy in which some stand higher for us than others."

Higher for us than others. It is so. For me there will never be another cat like Charles. With him I came nearer than I have ever been, or ever shall be, to bridging the gulf which divides us from the so-called dumb animals. Many of my happiest hours were spent in his company, for there was communion between us. He tried, as I did, to bridge the gulf; and I do not think I deceive myself if I say there were times when we came very near to it.

He was a faithful and gentle cat. For kindness and respect he returned an abundant love. I count myself well rewarded for any gentleness he had at my hands. . . .

In the midst of widespread human suffering the death of a cat may seem an unimportant matter. Those who are indifferent to animals or merely tolerate them will doubtless think so, but anyone who has intimately known and loved an animal and has been honored with that animal's friendship and devotion will, I believe, agree with me that it is not easy to bear the loss. We must leave it at that.

Charles lies buried in a quiet corner of a Berkshire garden, warmed by the sun. I like to think of him in celestial sunshine, among the honored cats of all time, exchanging views—who knows?—with Dr. Johnson's Hodge on the relative merits of biscuits and oysters. And, as I think of him, I find it easy to agree with Bernard Shaw's Androcles that a heaven in which there are no animals would be a poor place indeed.

To a Siamese Cat

MICHAEL JOSEPH
(JUNE 1930–DECEMBER 1942)

I shall walk in the sun alone
    Whose golden light you loved:
    I shall sleep alone
And, stirring, touch an empty place:
I shall write uninterrupted
(Would that your gentle paw
Could stay my moving pen just once again!).

I shall see beauty
But none to match your living grace:
I shall hear music
But not so sweet as the droning song
With which you loved me.

I shall fill my days
But I shall not, cannot forget:
Sleep soft, dear friend,
For while I live you shall not die.

Prayer for a Little Kitten

RUTH M. OUTWATER
1952

 HOPE—AMONG those golden streets—
There is a grassy way
With bushes growing here and there
Where my little cat can play.
I hope there is an apple tree,
Like the one she had down here,
On which to sharpen her tiny claws
And climb away from fear.
I hope she gets her daily cream
In a dish that smells like home
And that she finds a friendly door
Wherever she may roam.
I hope there is a loving hand
To stroke her grey striped fur,
And—please—don't let her miss me, Lord,
The way I'm missing her!

The Fireside Sphinx (excerpt)

AGNES REPPLIER

1901

 HERE IS A sweet and sunny corner of the Elysian fields, where drowse and play, and drowse and play forever, a little band of cats, whose names, imperishable as their masters', are household words today. We know them well, these gentle furry ghosts, lifted to immortality by the human hands that fondled them in life. We know the white Muezza whom Mohammed loved, and Bouhaki of Thebes, proudest of his proud race, and Dick Whittington's thrice famous cat that made his master's fortune. We know this sleek and shining tortoise-shell, for she is Selima, fair and ill-fated, whom the glint of gold-fish tempted to her grave. This pensive pussy with clear topaz eyes shared Petrarch's heart with Laura; this splendid beast, Micetto, the sovereign Pontiff's gift; and his no less arrogant companion sat, it is whispered, by the side of Wolsey, when the butcher's son was Chancellor of England.

Montaigne's grey cat is here, indolently supercilious as in old earthly days; and Victor Hugo's Chanoine, the sleepiest puss in Paradise; and Baudelaire's mysterious pet, with pale fire gleaming 'neath his half-shut lids; and Moumoutte Blanche and Moumoutte Chinoise, rivals for M. Loti's fluctuating affections, and the superb dynasties, both white and black, that ruled for years over M. Gautier's heart and home. Here, too, is "great Atossa," sung into fame by Mr. Arnold; and that sedate and serious tabby who slept too long in Cowper's bureau drawer. And—honoured of all their race—here are two happy and distinguished cats whom we cannot remember without envy, nor name without respect,—Dr. Johnson's Hodge, and Hinse of Hinsefeld, the wise companion of Sir Walter Scott.

Into this august assembly, into this sacred circle, I fain in moments of temerity would introduce a little shade who stole too soon from the warm sun, and from the simple joys of life. She was dearly loved and early lost, and the scanty honours years of toil have brought me I lay at her soft feet for entrance fee. May Hodge and Hinse champion her cause with the Immortals for the sake of the unfaltering love I have ever borne their masters, and may her grace and beauty win for her what my poor pen is powerless to attain! Dear little ghost, whose memory has never faded from my heart, accept this book, dedicated to thee, and to all thy cherished race. Sleep sweetly in the fields of asphodel, and waken, as of old, to stretch thy languid length, and purr thy soft contentment to the skies. I only beg, as one before me begged of her dead darling, that, midst the joys of Elysium, I may not be wholly forgotten.

> *"Nor, though Persephone's own Puss you be,*
> *Let Orcus breed oblivion of me."*

The Epitaph of Felis
JOHN JORTIN
1757

The Epitaph of Felis
Who departed this life in the year 1757,
at the age of 14 years, 11 months and 4 days.

 MOST GENTLE *of cats through long-drawn*
sickness aweary,
Bidding a last farewell, turn to the waters below.
Quietly smiling to me says Queen Prosperpina, "Welcome!
Thine are the groves of the blest; thine the Elysian suns."
If I deserve so well, O merciful Queen of the Silent,
Let me come back one night, homeward returning again,
Crossing the threshold again in the ear of the master to
murmur,
"Even when over the Styx, Felis is faithful to thee."

In Memoriam Mrs. Snowball Pat Paw

Louisa M. Alcott
1868

THE PUBLIC BEREAVEMENT

T IS OUR painful duty to record the sudden and mysterious disappearance of our cherished friend, Mrs. Snowball Pat Paw. This lovely and beloved cat was the pet of a large circle of warm and admiring friends; for her beauty attracted all eyes, her graces and virtues endeared her to all hearts, and her loss is deeply felt by the whole community.

When last seen, she was sitting at the gate, watching the butcher's cart; and it is feared that some villain, tempted by her charms, basely stole her. Weeks have passed, but no trace of her has been discovered; and we relinquish all hope, tie a black ribbon to her basket, set aside her dish, and weep for her as one lost to us for ever.

A Lament for S. B. Pat Paw

Louisa M. Alcott

 e mourn the loss of our little pet,
   And sign o'er her hapless fate.
   For never more by the fire she'll sit,
Nor play by the old green gate.

The little grave where her infant sleeps,
   Is 'neath the chestnut tree;
But o'er her grave we may not weep,
   We know not where it may be.

Her empty bed, her idle ball,
   Will never see her more;
No gentle tap, no loving purr
   Is heard at the parlour door.

Another cat comes after her mice,
   A cat with a dirty face;
But she does not hunt as our darling did,
   Nor play with her airy grace.

Her stealthy paws tread the very hall
  Where Snowball used to play
But she only spits at the dogs our pet
  So gallantly drove away.

She is useful and mild, and does her best,
  But she is not fair to see;
And we cannot give her your place, dear,
  Nor worship her as we worship thee.

Au Revoir to Smokey

Edith B. Spaulding
1952

 E'LL FOLD THEM *for a night of rest,—*
These little scrambling feet;
For never in our world again
They'll scamper down the street,
Or climb the curtain, claw the rug,
Or scratch the walnut chair.
Yet shall these little quiet feet
Pad up the golden stair?

So cold and still, so far beyond
All days and nights of strife,—
With silky fur still fluffed and soft,
And round eyes closed on life!
I sift the earth above you, but
Your winsomeness can't die;
And, somehow, Smokey, I believe
That this is not good-bye.

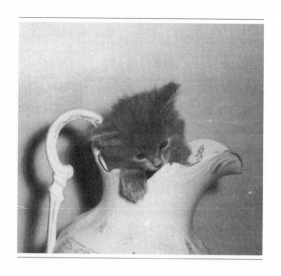

A heavenly mansion must have room
Somewhere among its halls,
For cushions where a little cat
May doze till Mistress calls.
And maybe, even at the door,
To make delight complete,
I'll hear above the harps the sound
Of little scrambling feet!

The Muse that Mewed

Wendy Wasserstein
1999

 DON'T COME from a long line of pet lovers. One of my earliest memories is of my mother, Lola, releasing our pet parakeet into a hurricane. She never explained how the bird flew out of her cage into the storm, but all we children knew it was involuntary. And then there was the time I came home from elementary school to find our newly acquired cocker spaniel on the roof. My mother promised me that the dog climbed up there for the view, but I certainly had never seen Lassie on the roof.

The police arrived, and the dog survived and subsequently moved to live with relatives in the suburbs. The last straw was my father driving a cat from our house in Brooklyn over the bridge into Manhattan and dropping her off somewhere near Wall Street, apparently hoping that a generous stockbroker would take her in or perhaps she would become a cub of the Dreyfus lion. Personally, I thought my entire family

should have been brought in for questioning by the animal rights board.

Ten years ago I advised a single friend of mine who was thinking about getting a dog that we had to try people first and then move on to animals. Within six months I had a cat, Ginger, and he a dog, Phyllis.

Ginger the cat had at least one life before she met me. I found her as an adult at the ASPCA and have no idea where she lived before. Ginger and I did not have love at first sight. In fact, it was my friend André who first spotted her. Actually it was André who dragged me to the ASPCA to begin with. He was a cat lover, the owner of the late, great Pussers, a gray aristocrat with elegant lines, and he convinced me to drop my fears of becoming L.S.W.W.C.—Lonely Single Woman with Cats—and replace them with the joy of having a warm, intelligent feline by the fire.

Ginger was never a calendar cat. We chose her because she was an orange calico, and if I was to have a cat I didn't want a czarina like Pussers but rather a fuzzy orange Creamsicle. My veterinarian, Dr. Ann Lucas, says Ginger was between 3 and 4 years old when we first met her and always had an older cat's teeth and personality. That was fine—frankly, I didn't want a Puffy jumping around the house with a ball of yarn.

I had read once in an Ann Beattie interview about her cats sitting on the windowsill as the light flooded in on a bright winter day as the delicate and talented writer sat down to work. I wanted old Ginger with her dark sad eyes seated beside me like a sheepdog as the evening light faded on my day's literary travels.

You can't always get what you want. Forget Puffy—

Ginger's voice and personality verged on Linda Blair's in *The Exorcist*. Unlike the millionaire singer kitty who croons about her love for chicken and liver, Ginger had a grating prolonged meow that sounded like Ethel Merman holding a note and belting, "I can do anything better than you." At any moment I thought her head would swivel and she would inform me that my mother sucked bad things that rhymed with clocks in hell. Every morning at five she would tap my head and hair until I served up her favorite turkey Fancy Feast. On four cans of Fancy Feast a day, sad-eyed Ginger and a furry Dallas Cowboys football soon became indistinguishable.

During my life with Ginger our personalities began to merge; Ginger preferred resting by the radiator to any physical activities, and so did I. Ginger believed all things could be solved by a snack and a phone call, and so did I. After the day's activities, I would call my neighbor Michi to chat, and Ginger would jump on the bed and pull on the phone cord. Finally, I began leaving messages for Aunt Michi from Ginger ranging from her thoughts on Socks the White House cat to her feline opinions of me.

During my life with Ginger, I wrote better and more happily than ever before. While I was at the desk, she didn't sit on the windowsill but on the bed. I would finish a scene, get on the bed to rest, and we would look it over together. I was 36 years old, writing my play *The Heidi Chronicles*, and she was probably 102, but I always thought of us as a girl and her cat. And at the end of a particularly satisfying Saturday evening at home in a Lanz flannel nightgown, I would watch Ginger's TV idol Toonces, the driving cat, on *Saturday Night Live*. Toonces was the feline version of George Maharis in *Route 66*. This kitty—not a computer actualization but a kitty as real as Ginger—got behind the wheel of his convertible weekly and took to the road. Ginger, who had never been impressed by the mention in *The Heidi Chronicles* (as the famous children's book *King Ginger the Lion*), sat on my lap for *Saturday Night Live* because our neighbor, her Aunt Michi, knew someone at the show and therefore could introduce her to Toonces.

Toonces died of cancer at age nine. Ginger died of bladder cancer at age 12 or maybe, according to Dr. Lucas, at 14. All I know is that both passed away at about the same time. I found out about Ginger's diagnosis while I was working on a play in London. As I look back on it, I was told I would have to fly to New York and close my Broadway play and my cat on the same weekend. I know plays have to close, but I had no idea I would be losing my companion, my best source of funny anecdotes, my friend through mostly thick and seldom thin. When Ginger had first arrived at my home, I wrote a song medley for her of Ginger's greatest hits—including "Rootilda," sung to "Matilda" using her nickname "Root," as in gingerroot. I had no idea that the pleasure of Ginger sitting on my stomach over the Sunday *Times* and our singing a duet of "Rootilda"—her Linda Blair falsetto and my Harry Belafonte—would become a memory. I was very jealous this past Christmas when I saw the MTV video of those caroling kitties. If only Ginger had survived two more months I could have been a stage mother.

Ginger was diagnosed for her final curtain in early July. She survived until November. Ginger, who developed a taste for not only Fancy Feast but the dramatic during her stay with me, had an *On Golden Pond* finale; I believe in the last months of her life Ginger fell in love.

A doctor I respect once told me that treating cancer is like chasing a fish: you watch where it swims and take it from there. Ginger certainly wasn't swimming upstream, but she wasn't drowning, either. While I had to be in London, I hired a handsome young man named Ken to move in with Ginger. Suddenly Ginger made a miraculous (albeit short-term) recovery— kidney counts were down and Kenny Cassillo was in the air. She followed him around the house and stared at him lovingly while he sat at the desk. At last, I had a son-in-law. Every week that summer, Cindy, my assistant, and beloved Kenny packed up Ginger and took her in a town car to Dr. Lucas. Ginger always traveled first-class. She was Orphan Annie—the cat who made it from the ASPCA to Fifth Avenue. No public transportation for her. At the end of her life she even switched from Fancy Feast to Hedleigh's Gourmet Shoppe sliced turkey.

During the fall, when I lived at home again, she became incontinent, but as long as her blood levels were acceptable and she wasn't in pain, I was still chasing that fish. Finally, in November while I was in Los Angeles for a week, Cindy called me to say she thought it was time.

Ken and I took Ginger down to Dr. Lucas for her final visit. She sat in my lap, now very thin and very sweet, and I lifted her to the window. "Look at the world, Ginger," I told her. I wanted her to know where she was leaving so she could tell stories where she was going.

I couldn't bear to go home that afternoon. I got back on a plane to Los Angeles and as I looked out the window at a flash of orange in the sky I thought of the Elton John song about Daniel waving good-bye; she was on her way to meet Toonces in his red convertible and drive to visit our friend Harry Kondoleon, the playwright who had been chasing an immune-deficiency fish for the past five years.

I imagined Harry greeting Ginger: "It's you. Come in. I have cans and cans of Fancy Feast. How is Wendy? Everyone up here knows you wrote all her plays."

And sometimes I think she did.

Epitaph for a Black Persian

E. B. CROSSWHITE

1930

 Y NOW, YOU'LL *have explored the Mansions*
of the
Blest and left dark clumps of fur on pearl-
and-jasper
Chairs. Upon the silken carpet of the Golden Stairs
You must have paused to sharpen claws with eager zest,
Whenever members of a seraph band divest themselves
Of the accouterments an angel wears, they surely find
You, later on, devoid of cares, ensconced inside a
Halo, as within a nest.

Perhaps St. Peter more than once has learned to smile,
As on his hand that holds the busy Judgment
Pen is suddenly your tongue, applied without finesse,
So like the stroking of a wet, persistent file—a
Touch I would that I might feel just once again—
Your own conception of an extra-fine caress.

Memoir for Mrs. Sullavan

BRYNA UNTERMEYER
1966

ONE MORNING in 1961, Louis was correcting typed sheets at his desk while I was working at the photocopies, finishing up the last section of a multivolume anthology for young people that we had been editing over a period of several years, when a long-distance call from Washington, D.C., came through. It was the Library of Congress asking if Louis would accept appointment as Consultant in Poetry for the 1961 to '62 period.

Louis's first reaction, after the initial glow of gratification, was that we could not possibly tear ourselves away from the cats, the house, our offices, our deadlines, and take up residence in Washington.

"We couldn't, could we?" he said wistfully.

"Of course we can. The cats are no problem. Weren't they fine last winter when we were away in the Mediterranean for seven weeks?"

"You're right," he said. "What about the dog?"

"Puck will go with us, of course."

"And the house?"

"Washington isn't Timbuktu. We can come home every month, every weekend, if we want."

"That's so. And I suppose mail can be forwarded."

"There's really nothing that we can't transfer."

"It might be exciting to be in Washington," Louis said.

"It will be marvelous!"

Once we had committed ourselves, the prospect seemed so irresistible that we couldn't credit our momentary hesitation. After years of our rural retreat, spending a season or two in "town"—especially a town as cosmopolitan but as open as the capital—appealed to us. The appointment came at exactly the right time. We were about to conclude the heavy commitment that had preoccupied us, and all signs and portent were most propitious. Elated, we set up a schedule: we had August and September in which to clear our desks, find an apartment near the Library, arrange a care-and-feeding-of-cats program, plan what to pack, what to take, what to leave, make endless lists of Things Not to Forget. The rest of the summer would flash by in a happy flurry.

And then Sullavan disappeared. She had greeted me in the morning as always, run upstairs to our bedroom as soon as I let her out of the kitchen, paced up the length of Louis to give him a good-morning butt, eaten an ample breakfast, and then wandered outside. Louis remembered seeing her weaving among the deep grasses of the orchard. During the middle of the afternoon it started to rain, at first a drizzle and then a soaking downpour from a heavily clouded sky. Cleo darted in from the screen porch as soon as the wind drove the wet through the mesh. Bobo came in through the hatch a few minutes later, his coat glistening with drops, followed by Plush with her fur pasted down on her head and back.

When Louis shut up shop for the day and crossed the road from his studio I was disappointed to see that he did not have Sullavan with him.

"The others came in out of the rain some time ago," I said. "I assumed Sullavan must be with you."

"No," he said, puzzled. "She hasn't been in the studio with me at all today. I wonder where she is."

"Sleeping, maybe, under a bush," I said.

"Probably," Louis said. "She often likes being out in the rain." Which was true. She often "rode out" a storm in some snug nest under a bush, to emerge as the rain dwindled, her coat only slightly damp, the moisture enhancing her personal perfume.

However, when she failed to put in an appearance at suppertime, we began to be more perturbed and went

to bed reminding ourselves that that other time, years ago, she had come back, that she would always come back.

She wasn't there in the morning. It was still raining. It looked as if we were in for an all-day rain. In overshoes and with umbrellas we went through the motions of walking up and down along the roads, calling her, whistling, penetrating into the rain-soaked fields as well as we were able to, finally giving up, drenched and discouraged, because it was impossible to cover every inch of ground; in which direction to search, in what thicket, under what tree, in which pasture might she be?

As the day wore on, all our smug satisfaction slipped away. I phoned all the neighbors. No one had seen her. We tried to work, to keep our minds away from conjecturing all the things that might have happened to her. By nightfall we were steeling ourselves to the worst, not only that Sullavan was dead, but that we might never know where or how she died.

The next morning we had so little hope that we took for granted she would not be there. The rain had ended; the sun shone; the roads and fields dried out. I covered the orchard once more, more to be doing something than with any expectation of finding her.

Then Louis and I forced ourselves to weed the flower beds; the soil was moist and yielding after the rain, and the physical activity eased us without making any demands on our dejection.

In the middle of the afternoon a little boy came to the front gate and called to us where we stooped at the task.

"Hey," he yelled. "Hey, mister, is that your cat up there in the road? There's a cat up there. Something's wrong with it."

Sullavan was sprawled at the side of the road. When we reached her she opened her eyes and then closed them again. She was breathing heavily. Her fur was matted and mud-streaked, and we saw that her left front paw was covered with dried blood. Louis stroked her before picking her up as carefully as he could. Though she moaned, she licked his hand.

He held her that way, cradled in his arms, all during the fifteen-minute ride to the hospital. We hardly spoke except once, when Louis said, "I knew if she was alive she would come home somehow."

Dr. Lubin told us that he thought Sullavan had been shot, and after he operated to clean out the wound, which was two days old and already in a state of degeneration, he said there was no question of it. A bullet had gone through the leg, smashing the bone to splinters. We raged futilely at the knowledge. It was no accident, no fight with another animal. A person was responsible; the chances were that it was one of the neighborhood boys, which one we would never know, taking potshots at anything that moved. Having succeeded in hitting her so neatly, he had left her to die in the woods.

The next day the report from the hospital was not too discouraging. Sullavan had come out of the anesthesia well; had taken a little milk, but was still running a fever. "You must understand," Dr. Lubin said, "that the problem is not only infection. There is the possibility of gangrene."

In twenty-four hours the gangrene was an actuality.

"It's going to be critical now," Dr. Lubin told us. "This is the situation: If the gangrene begins to spread, it will be the end, unless—you have one other choice—I can amputate. If I do it in time I may be able to save her. You have to make the decision. A lot of people can't see doing it. But I can assure you that if the cat survives she'll accommodate to three legs and get along fine. It's up to you. I have to know, though, because I may have to act quickly."

Louis and I didn't even have to look at each other. We said almost simultaneously, "Save her. If you can. Save her."

The following day Dr. Lubin phoned. "The gangrene is spreading. You still want me to go ahead?"

"Yes, yes," I wept. "Go ahead."

"Fine," he said. "I bet she'll come through it beautifully."

He called back in a few hours.

"She's doing nicely," he said. "I think we caught it in time."

The next report was most encouraging. Temperature gone, no indication of pain. Louis and I smiled at each other for the first time in four days. Sullavan was going to get better. We could feel it.

"It would be too cruel for her to have died like that," I said. "To have dragged herself home, from God knows how far off—it must have taken her two days to do it—and then to die now . . ."

Dr. Lubin called again. "The only thing that bothers me about her at the moment is she hasn't eaten. She won't eat. And she has to gain strength. I think what's indicated is that you come and feed her."

"Special food?"

"No, her regular food."

"Right away?"

"The sooner the better."

With a little container of chopped meats and a

queer nervousness in our stomachs, Louis and I presented ourselves at the veterinary hospital. I almost dreaded the moment of seeing Sullavan. I am often sharply distressed by disfigurements; at this point, I was not really confident of my own reactions. I suspect Louis felt something similar.

Prior to that day we had never been behind the scenes at the hospital, familiar though we were with the waiting and examining rooms. Somewhat gingerly we followed Dr. Lubin to the immaculate, disinfectant-smelling special-care ward. Sullavan's "room" was on the upper tier of cages, at eye level.

She was lying listlessly in the rear of the cage; her coat, I noticed at once, was dull and "staring." The whole cat looked shrunken. But our footsteps must have had a familiar ring to her, for she lifted her head at our approach. Over the lump in my throat I managed to call "Sulllll-a-vannn," low, the food call she knew so well. She purred, rose to her three legs, and tottered uncertainly toward us. We were so moved that we were embarrassed. Louis's eyes filled and overflowed; Dr. Lubin had, with considerable tact, left us alone.

We forced ourselves to study the amputation. It had been done with great skill, close to the body, so that there was no break in the smooth line of our cat's chest; a flap of fur had been concealingly sewn over the wound.

We didn't dare lift Sullavan out of the cage that day, but we petted her and fondled her and talked to her tenderly. Then we blew our noses and got down to the business of hand-feeding her. She took enough of the meat to encourage us.

"Tomorrow I'll bring kidneys for her," I told the doctor. "They're her favorite. Fresh, you know—I cut them up tiny. She likes them uncooked. I didn't have any in the refrigerator when you phoned, but I'll get some on the way back."

The kidneys were a great success. Sullavan ate with a show of normal appetite, and Dr. Lubin said that if she continued to do as well, and if we were willing to undertake the nursing that would be required, he would be inclined to let us take her home in several days.

"You'll have to bring her in to have stitches removed," he said, "but she'll be happier home and she'll eat better."

We assured Dr. Lubin fervently that we would go on twenty-four-hour nursing duty if necessary, just as long as we could take Sullavan home. Our eagerness was increased by a touching little byplay in the hospital, in which we had taken part.

On the first visit, all the other patients in Sullavan's ward, several cats and assorted dogs, crowded to the doors of their cages, whimpering, whining, mewing, yapping, as we fed her. We felt so guilty that, having asked permission, the second day we brought along enough kidneys to treat them all. To our astonishment, none of the animals would eat. As we realized poignantly, they weren't hungry for food; it was affection and attention they wanted and cried for. Sick as some of them were, what they envied Sullavan was our presence and our petting, not our provisions. Kind words were better than kidneys.

We took Sullavan home at the earliest possible moment, installing her in my studio, where she would not be molested or disturbed by the other animals. With her own indoor toilet and a cozy bed, she settled down to a contented convalescence, gaining strength and luster every day. She drowsed most of the time; we took turns holding her in our laps for long, loving spells, to reassure her and give her confidence; and when she asked to go out, one or the other of us walked beside her in her halting progress. The first few airings we picked her up before she could tire herself. It was impossible to know how well she would understand her own handicap. How could she protect herself or escape if she met an enemy? We did not dare leave her outside alone.

In fact, we did not see how we could leave her at all. It was the end of August. Inevitably we decided not only that there was no alternative but to take her to Washington with us but that we would be miserable with worry were we to be at any distance from her. In her present condition, we concluded, she would not suffer from confinement in an apartment.

All of this changed completely in another week. Each day she moved more easily, more rapidly; each day she ate more and slept less, until she was sufficiently restored to do what we would not have believed she would ever do again: she leaped the front fence! Once we saw that, we realized that she was able to be on her own once more. Our determination to take her to Washington began to dissipate. When she brought home a bird a few days later, we gave in. If she wanted to convince us that she was restored and was entitled to remain free-roaming, she had succeeded. Not that we were completely serene about her. She had become pitifully light in our arms, as though she were a hollow cat, all pretty fur and frailty.

September 30, the day before we were to drive

down to Washington, was a teaser of a day, one of those perfect days of early fall when the sun blows warm and the breeze blows cool, a day calculated to make us wonder if where we were going could be half as delightful as what we were leaving. Directly after lunch I left to do last-minute chores in the village. Louis was puttering around the flower beds, doing last-minute weeding. Sullavan was curled up in a weeding basket—during the last few weeks she had reverted to her infant fondness for baskets—and we had been playfully moving the basket along with the sun, so that it was truly, we said, a basking basket.

An hour later I returned home. As I drove the car into the garage, Louis came out to meet me.

"There's bad news," he said gently. "Sullavan is dead."

I was stunned.

"The last time I looked," Louis continued painfully, "she was still sleeping in the basket. But a few minutes ago I noticed her lying on the lawn below the back terrace. It seemed odd, and when I went over to her she was dead, with a dead bird in her paws. There's a froth of blood on her mouth, but nothing else. She looks normal, no sign of pain—she looks happy. She must have had a hemorrhage as she caught the bird, and died in that instant."

We sadly wrapped her in cloth and carried her to the orchard, picking a spot under one of the largest trees that I particularly loved, where the grass grows silky and long like fairy grass. We took turns digging the small grave. After we covered her with soil, we placed three large flat stones on the grave to protect it and mark it. Both of us were weeping all the time.

"I'm glad she didn't die in the woods or in the hospital," I said. "This was a happy way for her to die."

We were grateful to leave the next day and to be gone for a while. There were too many things in our house that would have reminded us of Sullavan.

There still are.

Walking With Lulu in the Wood

NAOMI LAZARD
1969

T HE WOOD *is a good place to find*
The other road down to that hollow
Which rocks a little with the same
Motion as my soul. Come on, Lulu,
Follow me and be careful of the rain
Washed leaves. But you were always gentle.
I'll be quiet too, and we won't disturb
The raccoons or any of the other animals.
I want to talk with the God here, Lulu.
This is a grove where he must be hiding,
And here is a pool for small water god
To swim in. Let's talk with the god, Lulu.

The sun makes a great splash and you
Are the one who is hiding in the tall grass
Just the way you used to Lulu,
You are the color of sand in a certain light,
Like the shadow of light. The sun
Is embracing me; the shadow also
means death. It is the god's word

In the language he speaks. He says
you are small again, that you have chosen it.
He says your reflection will be in the pool
Forever, a blue resemblance, a startled joy.
He says this is your world now, this night
Of tall trees, this cave of silences.
He says he loves you too; he watches you sleep.

Is the grove real? Is this your heaven, Lulu,
That you have let me enter? This glade,
The winter ivories?—the season you missed
By dying in the fall. Are these your jeweled
stones, your curled-up animals, your grass?
And your god, the secret splash in the water
That you always seemed to be listening for?
Is it the god's way—the mouth in the wood,
The opening to paradise?

God of animals and children, separations, loss.
Goodbye. Goodbye, sweet girl, again.
The days pass like oranges tossed
From hand to hand. Then one will drop
And it will be my turn. Wait for me here.
I hope to be fortunate, to come back and share
This winter wood with you, the dark hollow,
The snow-dusted face of the god.

PET LOSS RESOURCES

Pet Loss Support Groups

A *Directory of Pet Loss Resources* listing pet loss counselors, telephone hotlines, and support groups throughout the United States is available from the Delta Society, 289 Perimeter Road East, Renton, WA 98055-1329, (425) 226–7357 (www.deltasociety.org).

Changes: The Support for People and Pets Program provides counseling, education, and research on pet loss. Memorial donations are accepted. Colorado State University Veterinary Teaching Hospital, 300 West Drake Rd., Fort Collins, CO 80523.

Pet Loss Support Hotline

University of California, Davis, Pet Loss Support Hotline, (530) 752–4200, 6:30–9:30 P.M. Monday through Friday, Pacific time. Pet loss support hotlines are also available at other veterinary schools throughout the United States.

Published Pet Memorials

Memorials are published in *Best Friends* magazine, or on the Best Friends website (www.bestfriends.org) with a donation to Best Friends Animal Sanctuary, Kanab, UT 84741; (801) 644–2001.

On the Internet

Rainbow Bridge Tribute Pages:
www.bestfriends.org
Pet Loss Grief Support Page and Candle Ceremony:
www.petloss.com
Virtual Pet Cemetery:
www.mycemetery.com
Association for Pet Loss and Bereavement:
www.aplb.org
In Memory of Pets Tribute Page:
www.in-memory-of-pets.com
CatOwner.com (a variety of resources on cats including news-groups, cat health, cat poetry and humor, and pet loss resources):
www.catowner.com

Recommended Reading

Deborah Antinori. *Journey Through Pet Loss*. Basking Ridge, NJ: YokoSpirit Publications, 1998 (audiotape and extensive resource list).

Gary Kowalski. *Goodbye Friend: Healing Wisdom for Anyone Who Has Ever Lost a Pet*. Walpole, NH: Stillpoint Publishing, 1997.

Cynthia Rylant. *Cat Heaven*. New York: Scholastic Books, 1997 (children's book).

Wallace Sife, Ph.D. *The Loss of a Pet*. New York: Howell Book House, 1998.

Susan Chernak McElroy. *Animals as Guides for the Soul: Stories of Life-Changing Encounters*. New York: Ballantine Books, 1998.

ACKNOWLEDGMENTS

THE SAYING that "pets bring people together" was demonstrated many times in the process of compiling this book. I am grateful to the friends and pet lovers who supported my efforts in so many ways: suggesting poems and stories; locating vintage photographs of cats; preparing the manuscript; and offering advice and encouragement throughout the process. Special thanks are due to Victoria Coulter, John King, Randy Varney, Alice Meerson, and Martine Helwig for always being there when I needed you. Thanks are also due to George and Sue Whiteley for sharing their treasured collection of vintage cat photographs. Dr. Alice Villalobos, a gifted healer of animals, is a continuing source of inspiration to me for her tireless work in promoting the human-animal bond. Maureen O'Brien, my editor at Hyperion, and her able assistants, Jennifer Morgan and Natalie Kaire, have guided this project from concept to completion and have taught me so much in the process. Finally, I am grateful to all of the pets who have taught me so many important lessons about the circle of life that we all share, and that even in loss there are many gifts.

BIBLIOGRAPHY

George Abbe. "Remembered Cat." *Saturday Review of Literature*, 1945. Used by permission of General Media Publishing Group.

Louisa May Alcott. "In Memoriam Mrs. Snowball Pat Paw." In *Little Women*, 1868.

Cleveland Amory. "L'Envoi." In *The Best Cat Ever*. Boston: Little, Brown and Co., 1993. Used by permission.

Anonymous. "The Rainbow Bridge." Date unknown.

Bianca Bradbury. "First Day in Heaven." *Household*, 1946.

Margaret E. Bruner. "Sonnet." In *Our Dumb Animals*, n.d. Used by permission of *Animals Magazine*.

Jean Burden. "A Leavetaking." *Woman's Day*, 1972. Used by permission of the author.

Louis J. Camuti. "Tailless Tom." In *All My Patients are Under the Bed*. New York: Simon & Schuster, 1985. Used by permission.

E. B. Crosswhite. "Epitaph for a Black Persian." *Saturday Evening Post*, 1930. Used by permission.

Lynn Hamilton. "Katinka." In *Sophisti-Cats, Poems for Cat Lovers*, ed. by Lynn Hamilton. Boston: Chapman and Grimes, 1952.

Thomas Hardy. "Last Words to a Dumb Friend." In *The Complete Poems of Thomas Hardy*, ed. James Gibson. New York: Macmillan, 1978. Used by permission.

Frances Minturn Howard. "Death of the Black Cat, Mr. Jingles." *Yankee Magazine*, 1958. Used by permission.

Constance Jenkins. "Request from the Rainbow Bridge." Copyright © 1992 by Constance Jenkins. Used by permission.

John Jortin. "The Epitaph of Felis." Original source unknown. In *The Poetical Cat, an Anthology*, ed. by Felicity Bast. New York: Farrar Straus Giroux, 1995.

Michael Joseph. *Charles, the Story of a Friendship* (excerpt). New York: Prentice-Hall, 1952.

Naomi Lazard. "Walking With Lulu in the Wood." *The New Yorker*, January 18, 1969. Used by permission of the author.

Gayle McCafferty. "Remembering Baggins." *Best Friends Magazine*, July/August 1999. Used by permission of the author.

Ruth M. Outwater. "Prayer for a Little Kitten." Hamilton, *Sophisti-Cats: Poems for Cat Lovers*.

Robert Peterson. "Calling Muzi." Copyright © 1987 by Robert Peterson. Used by permission.

Edna Dean Proctor. "My Grandmother's Cat." In *Cat Encounters; a Cat Lover's Anthology*, selected by Seon Manley and Gogo Lewis. New York: Lothrup, Lee & Shepard, 1979.

Agnes Repplier. *The Fireside Sphinx* (excerpt). Boston: Houghton, Mifflin, 1901.

Christina Rossetti. "On the Death of a Cat, a Friend of Mine Aged Ten Years and a Half." In *In Praise of Cats: an Anthology*. Dorothy Foster, comp. Ontario, Canada: Musson Book Co., 1974.

Clinton Scollard. "Grimalkin: An Elegy on Peter." In *Concerning Cats, My Own and Some Others* by Helen M. Winslow. Boston: Lothrop Publishing Co., 1900.

Henry Dwight Sedgwick. "Leo to His Mistress." *Atlantic Monthly*, n.d.

Margaret Sherwood. "In Memoriam: Leo, a Yellow Cat." *Atlantic Monthly*, 1913.

Edith B. Spaulding, "Au Revoir to Smokey." Hamilton, *Sophisti-Cats: Poems for Cat Lovers*.

Graham R. Tomson. "Dedication." In *Concerning Cats*. London: T. Fisher Unwin, 1892.

Bryna Untermeyer. *Memoir for Mrs. Sullavan*. New York: Simon & Schuster, 1966. Used by permission.

Carl Van Vechten. "Feathers." In *Sacred and Profane Memories*. New York: Alfred Knopf, 1932.

Randolph Varney. "Love, Squared." Copyright © 1999 by Randolph Varney. Used by permission.

Charles Dudley Warner. "Calvin: A Study of Character." In *My Summer in a Garden*. Boston: Houghton, Mifflin, 1882.

Wendy Wasserstein. "The Muse that Mewed." In *Animal Fair*, Premiere Issue, 1999. Used by permission of the author.

Clement Wood. "Purr Box." Hamilton, *Sophisti-Cats: Poems for Cat Lovers*.